blue
rider
press

THE END
OF NORMAL

THE END
OF NORMAL

A Wife's Anguish, A Widow's New Life

STEPHANIE MADOFF MACK

with Tamara Jones

BLUE RIDER PRESS

a member of Penguin Group (USA) Inc.

New York

blue
rider
press

Published by the Penguin Group
Penguin Group (USA) Inc., 375 Hudson Street, New York, New York 10014, USA ·
Penguin Group (Canada), 90 Eglinton Avenue East, Suite 700, Toronto, Ontario M4P 2Y3,
Canada (a division of Pearson Penguin Canada Inc.) · Penguin Books Ltd, 80 Strand,
London WC2R 0RL, England · Penguin Ireland, 25 St Stephen's Green, Dublin 2, Ireland
(a division of Penguin Books Ltd) · Penguin Group (Australia), 250 Camberwell Road,
Camberwell, Victoria 3124, Australia (a division of Pearson Australia Group Pty Ltd) ·
Penguin Books India Pvt Ltd, 11 Community Centre, Panchsheel Park, New Delhi–110 017, India ·
Penguin Group (NZ), 67 Apollo Drive, Rosedale, North Shore 0632, New Zealand (a division of
Pearson New Zealand Ltd) · Penguin Books (South Africa) (Pty) Ltd, 24 Sturdee Avenue,
Rosebank, Johannesburg 2196, South Africa

Penguin Books Ltd, Registered Offices: 80 Strand, London WC2R 0RL, England

ISBN 978-0-399-15816-2

Printed in the United States of America
1   3   5   7   9   10   8   6   4   2

BOOK DESIGN BY CLAIRE NAYLON VACCARO

While the author has made every effort to provide accurate telephone numbers and Internet
addresses at the time of publication, neither the publisher nor the author assumes any responsibility
for errors, or for changes that occur after publication. Further, the publisher does not have any
control over and does not assume any responsibility for author or third-party websites or their
content.

*Penguin is committed to publishing works of quality and integrity.
In that spirit, we are proud to offer this book to our readers;
however, the story, the experiences, and the words
are the author's alone.*

For my children,
Audrey and Nicholas,

and in loving memory of my husband,
Mark D. Madoff

CONTENTS

One · The Last Day of Normal   *1*

Two · Big Fish   *21*

Three · Becoming a Madoff   *47*

Four · Optical Illusions   *75*

Five · The Book of Ruth   *103*

Six · Riptide   *125*

Seven · December 2010   *159*

Eight · No More Lies   *181*

Nine · Our Own Good-bye   *203*

Ten · Wish Flowers   *231*

Epilogue   *237*

Acknowledgments   *251*

THE END
OF NORMAL

one

THE LAST DAY
OF NORMAL

Every night before going to sleep, I put a fresh towel down on my side of the bed, knowing it will be drenched with perspiration by the time I bolt awake, precisely and without fail, at 3:51 in the morning. Usually I'm sobbing already, my body shaking, my heart exploding. I don't know this person, this scared new self. I wish I could believe even once that she isn't real, that I'm seeing her through the fog of a bad dream. I was always the one who would nod off three pages into a book, or before the first commercial if Mark and I were watching TV after the kids were down for the night. Mark used to joke about how soundly I could sleep, how utterly peaceful I looked, and how loudly I could snore. Now night terrors have become my normal.

How cruel that they would begin in a place that once felt so safe and comforting, so alive with our happiness. By day, our apartment on Mercer Street was airy and inviting, a signature SoHo loft with soaring ceilings and a full wall of windows. Mark and I loved the big, open floor plan, and we had eagerly knocked down more walls to make it even more expansive. I never imagined that there would come a time when our beautiful home would close in on me deep in the night, sucking the air from my lungs, waking me in a panic.

Now it doesn't matter where I am anymore: The terror will find me. I know I will lie there crying in the predawn hush, my children in their cartoon pajamas sleeping unaware in their bedrooms down the hall. Filled with dread, I follow what has become a horrifying ritual. I wrap my fingers around my throat and tighten my grip gradually, testing. How long do the lungs fight back? I imagine the moment when everything goes black. Is there a rush of pain, of fear, or is it euphoric relief?

I turn onto my left side to stare at the alarm clock on the nightstand, willing the glowing numbers to fall into place. I need it to be time. I need it to be 4:14. There is a reason why I am awake at this hour, a vigil I have to keep.

And so I watch the clock, silently counting off the same twenty-three minutes night after night, waiting for my husband to kill himself.

By the time the first morning light spills through the window, I am able to be the person the world needs me to be again, finishing my cup of tea, getting both kids ready for preschool, checking my e-mail to determine what needs to be done and who can't be ignored. I follow the *Hallmark Hall of Fame* script of a lucky stay-at-home mother, ordering cupcake slippers for my daughter online, signing up for a spin class at the gym, making plans to meet an old friend for a glass of wine before dinner. I apologize to the dog as he whimpers in front of the cabinet where his treats are stored. "You've already had enough."

If you were outside looking in on this tableau, you might think we were any normal family. You might think we were more than content, living a dream life, even. You would be wrong. But we were that, and we had that, once.

Our last day of normal fell in the winter of 2008. It was December, and we were in Greenwich, Connecticut, where we spent every Tuesday night with Mark's two children from his first marriage. It seems like I should be able to remember what we talked about that night, what news the kids had about their classmates or their tennis lessons or swim meets, the table manners we corrected or sibling quarrels we quashed. But these banalities of everyday life aren't anything you think to preserve, much less cherish. Why bother? It was just another Tuesday.

The next morning, December 10, we drove the kids to school before heading back to Manhattan. Mark rolled down his window as usual to heckle his thirteen-year-old daughter as she joined a clutch of friends heading to class. "Hey, Kate! Learn a lot!" he shouted, laughing when she shot him the mortified look he had hoped for. Mark worshipped Kate and her sixteen-year-old brother, Daniel, with a devotion I found alternately endearing and maddening. His kids came

first, no matter what. As a parent, I understood that part of the equation perfectly. But Mark also had a chronic case of divorced-daddy
syndrome, missing his son and daughter so much that he often over-
compensated by trying to anticipate every possible need and kowtow
to every whim. When we were all together, any restaurant we ate at
or movie we saw was the children's choice to make. Mark craved their
company, but now that they were teenagers, Kate and Daniel both had
busy social lives of their own to manage, and that didn't always include blocking out Tuesday nights or every other weekend for their
father. It didn't matter. Even if he knew he wouldn't see them, Mark
insisted that we make the hour-long trip just so they would know he
was there.

Try as I did to be a good sport—and a good stepmother—I have
to admit that being a second wife grated on me at times, and my inse-
curities about my own place in the pecking order of Mark's close-knit
family were the biggest bone of contention between the two of us.
It wasn't just my imagination, though. I was often overshadowed by
Mark's failed first marriage, so much so that his mother routinely
called me Susan instead of Stephanie, even though I had come along
three years after his bitter divorce. It rankled me that Kate and Daniel's mother remained, by extension, so deeply entwined in our lives.
"It's part of the mix," Mark would shrug, anxious to keep the peace.
I tried to suck it up, and was successful more often than not, but I
never really perfected the art.

Despite the challenges of a blended family, our marriage had found its sweet spot, and that December I was seven months pregnant with our second child. A little brother for our daughter, Audrey, who had just turned two. A very active little brother, if the kickboxing sessions in utero were any indication. We debated names that morning on our drive back to the city: Nicholas or Joe? We were still torn. Audrey was in her car seat, blissing out over a strawberry-frosted doughnut with rainbow sprinkles. In the cargo hold, our shamefully spoiled Labradoodle, Grouper, dozed in the dog bed I had bought especially for road trips. The lack of squirrels to chase in SoHo always put Grouper in a sulk on the way home.

As usual, I claimed control of the radio dial for the commute, quickly nixing Mark's soft-rock preferences for a Top 40s mix. Taste in music was one of the rare differences that underscored our ten-year age gap, and I refused to be the enabler of someone who wanted to linger forever at some 1980s high school prom. I teased Mark about it mercilessly, but he held fast to his romanticism, and truth be told, it was pretty charming. He always knew how to make me laugh. Once, after I had won yet again in our power struggle over who got to be deejay, Mark fired off an e-mail to my iPhone minutes after dropping me off somewhere. I opened it to find a picture of the car's radio console, triumphantly displaying the call numbers of Mark's favorite XM station, The Heart, which played nothing but lovesick ballads. Had it been left to Mark, we might have ended up with Barry Manilow's "Can't Smile Without You" as our wedding dance.

If easy listening was Mark's cheesy weakness, then Christmas was mine. I'm a sucker for every sentimental movie, nostalgic decoration, and Rockwellian moment the holiday season has to offer. Knit reindeer hats can be found in my closet—and I actually wear them. As a child growing up in New York, some of my fondest memories are of Christmastime, when December turned the grimy city into a big enchanted snow globe. You could be walking down Fifth Avenue and come across a Juilliard quartet playing "O Come, All Ye Faithful" on a street corner, and the taxi-honking, bus-wheezing, brake-screeching cacophony of the evening rush hour would suddenly hold still. In Central Park, skaters twirled and tumbled across the vast frozen pond, and the rich, smoky smell of roasting chestnuts would make your eyes sting and your mouth water.

Best of all were the big department stores like Macy's and Lord & Taylor in full holiday glory, trying to outdo one another with their magical Christmas windows. I would stand outside on the sidewalk, mesmerized by the animated elves busily making toys in Santa's workshop, or the tender beauty of a Victorian doll family in exquisite period costumes, waltzing around a candlelit tree. I could never drink in enough of the season. Every year, my parents would take my brother and me to buy a Christmas tree from a stand in front of a private girls' school on 91st Street, a few blocks from our apartment. A portion of the tree sales went to charity, and my stepdad, Marty, loved to tease my brother and me by feigning horror at the outrageous prices and then picking out the tiniest, scrawniest Charlie Brown tree he could find. My mother would then make a great show of putting her foot down, and ultimately we would lug home a big, magnificent tree, which we would decorate while listening to the Supremes singing Christmas songs. There were beautiful heirloom ornaments my mother had had as a little girl, and handcrafted ones my aunt lovingly made each year, crocheting snowflakes from delicate white yarn or turning clothespins into toy soldiers. My favorite was the ice-cream cone she made using a big hot-pink pom-pom for the scoop.

Mark was Jewish, but his parents had never been observant, and he eagerly embraced my Christmas traditions when we became a couple. Still, I was fearful of offending anyone in his family, so I started the tradition of hosting a big Hanukkah party for Bernie, Ruth, and the children. I made sure the kids all got gifts from us for both holidays. Between that and Audrey's birthday, I generally spent the fall in a perpetual state of frenzied wrapping. With the new baby on the way that year, though, I'd finished my gift shopping months in advance. We'd gotten our tree the week before and trimmed it, too. It was the first year that Audrey was old enough to get excited about it, and watching her squeal over some of my own childhood ornaments had been one of those special motherhood moments for me. With all of the prep work out of the way early, I was really looking forward to just taking it easy and enjoying the festivities with my little family.

After inching our way through midtown traffic that Wednesday morning, Mark pulled the SUV over as we neared the red-granite Lipstick Building, where he worked at his father's brokerage firm. Bernie was a titan in the financial world, a widely admired former president of NASDAQ. A glassed-in office at Bernard L. Madoff Investment Securities commanded respect. At forty-four years old, having worked for his father his entire adult life, Mark was proud to have earned his spot as a senior manager on the nineteenth floor of the market-making segment at the firm. He had never had any doubts that this was where he belonged, and he had never known anything else.

"Talk to you later, kitten," he promised as he jumped out onto Third Avenue and I maneuvered my pregnant belly behind the steering wheel. We had the company's annual holiday party to attend that night at a popular Mexican restaurant the firm had rented out for the bash. Reluctant as I was to keep buying maternity clothes so close to my due date, the party was reason enough for me to splurge on a festive top to go with my standard dark "going out" maternity jeans. Too bad pregnancy had made me such a major party pooper—I was wiped out by eight o'clock most evenings—but I was still looking forward to having a fun time, even if the margaritas were off-limits for me now. The Wall Street crowd knew how to blow off steam, especially the young traders. It was bound to be loud and lively. And my in-laws would be there, too, of course.

Though we saw each other often, I was especially curious to see what kind of mood they would be in that night. Both had been acting strange lately, and Mark suspected that his father might be hiding a serious illness from the family. He just wasn't himself. The last time Bernie had behaved this way was when Mark's younger brother, Andy, had been diagnosed with lymphoma a few years back. Andy had fought his illness with quiet courage and a strong will, but Bernie had fallen apart at the word *cancer* and had barely been able to function throughout Andy's treatment.

Now Bernie seemed unhinged again, and both Mark and Andy, who also worked at the firm, were worried. Their mother seemed somewhat anxious and preoccupied, too. Bernie was nearing seventy and was an unhealthy eater; he often had a pack of those orange fake-cheese and peanut butter crackers in his pocket and never exercised. Mark loved to tell the story of his father getting a sudden spurt of motivation and climbing onto the treadmill that Ruth had in her home gym. Bernie hadn't gotten far when his sneakers began to literally disintegrate on his feet because the rubber on the soles was so old and dry. He hadn't replaced them in at least twenty years. Just what kind of shape Bernie was in was hard to say, though. His phobia of doctors prevented him from making an appointment for even a routine physical, much less a full workup. For a few weeks now, Mark and his brother had watched Bernie sitting in his glass office at the Lipstick Building, staring at the ceiling all day.

"What do you mean 'all day'?" I initially pressed Mark when he had brought it up at home after a troubling day at work.

"Steph, I don't know," he said with a sigh. "I think he's very sick, or maybe dying."

Usually, Bernie spent his workdays glued to the phone, ushering important investors into and out of his office, and intently monitoring every twitch, shudder, and surge on his trading room floor. Now, Mark said, he seemed completely disinterested. Attempts at conversation were met with monosyllabic responses, and when Mark asked him what was going on, Bernie insisted nothing was wrong. But something definitely was.

I had witnessed Bernie's odd behavior for myself soon after, when I dropped by the office with Audrey so we could all go out to celebrate her second birthday with a family lunch and a trip to FAO Schwarz afterward. A friend had given Audrey a gift certificate to make her own Muppet at the famous toy store, and I knew her grandparents would want to share the fun. Ruth kept an office in Bernie's fiefdom, too, where she ostensibly managed the family charitable foundation. Usually, when I showed up with Audrey, Bernie and Ruth couldn't drop their work fast enough to smother their youngest grandchild with attention. For her birthday, they had really gone overboard; they bought Audrey a fully outfitted pink kitchen from Pottery Barn Kids, complete with every accessory the store had to offer, from the miniature rolling pin and the tiny pot holders to a gazillion pieces of fake food. Whenever Audrey was around, there was no question at all that she was the center of their universe. That November 21, though, as we stood waiting expectantly outside Bernie's office, we may as well have been standing on Mount Kilimanjaro. There was Bernie, sitting at his desk, eyes fixed on the ceiling just as Mark had described, his head thrown back, his hands steepled beneath his chin, still as a sculpture. He didn't look lost in deep thought—he just looked blank.

"Shit, I see what you mean now," I murmured to Mark as we stood outside Bernie's office. "He looks so strange."

Soon Ruth appeared and fussed over Audrey, and Bernie finally snapped out of his spell and ambled out to greet us. But as we got ready to head to the restaurant, Bernie hung back.

"You're not coming with us?" I asked. Bernie said something

vague about being too busy and retreated to his office as we left. Begging off a granddaughter's birthday lunch might seem minor, but for Bernie it was completely out of character.

Audrey's party at a kids' gym the next day was equally unsettling on the grandparent front. Ruth and Bernie not only never missed a family get-together, they usually arrived early. And if they were coming in from Palm Beach or Europe, it could be *hours* early, and by private jet, no less, so it wasn't as if they worried about traffic. They were just that eager to see their grandchildren. I had to remind myself that overbearing was better than uninterested, and even if they popped in on us a couple of hours early, I was grateful that my kids would grow up knowing they were absolutely beloved by their grandparents on both sides of the family. I could live with Ruth and Bernie's eccentricities.

But as Audrey's birthday party got under way that Saturday, Ruth and Bernie were nowhere to be seen. When they finally arrived twenty minutes late, Ruth confided that Bernie had collapsed on the sidewalk outside a SoHo store where they'd gone to return some clothing. He was fine, they both insisted, but I could tell that Ruth, at least, was rattled.

My parents and Bernie sat down with the rest of the adults to watch the kids enjoy themselves, but Ruth hurtled herself into the middle of the toddler mayhem. It wasn't unusual for her to be the life of the party, but seeking that spotlight at a kiddie playdate was extreme even by Ruth's standards. The rest of us watched in dismay as she jumped into the big pit full of foam balls and began cavorting with the two-year-olds. There was something more frantic than funny about it. My mother, known to her friends as Pinks, occasionally socialized with the Madoffs. After the party, she told me she'd sensed an undercurrent of desperation in Ruth, as if she were trying to prove what a good grandmother she was, when nobody doubted it in the first place. In hindsight, I have to wonder whether my mom's instincts were right: Ruth definitely wanted to leave an impression that day.

Part of me wondered why the Madoffs weren't showing the same wild enthusiasm for the grandson I was carrying that fall; reaction to the imminent arrival of Joe-or-Nicholas so far had been subdued, even when Mark proudly told his parents that his son would carry the middle name of Bernie's father, Ralph. We thought they would be touched, but Ruth just scoffed and Bernie said nothing.

The baby's nursery was still unfinished, and my good friend Susan, a brilliant interior designer, was planning on meeting me at our apartment with a contractor after I dropped Mark off at work that Wednesday morning. We wanted to sketch out where the baby furniture would go and design custom shelving that would be able to carry a little boy through childhood, from teddy bears to football trophies. Our meeting had barely gotten under way when my phone vibrated. Mark was calling. I let it go to voice mail; he would call back if it was important. It immediately vibrated again. When I picked it up, Mark sounded agitated.

"Where are you?" He was out of breath, barely able to get the words out. I was instantly scared.

"What's wrong?" I asked.

"Just tell me where you are right now."

"I'm at home. I'm having that meeting about the baby's room." Mark sounded angry, and I could tell now that he was hyperventilating. I walked away from the baby's room, into the office off of our living room, and closed the door behind me. "Are you all right? Please tell me you're all right!" Mark didn't answer. I heard him catching his breath again.

"You need to get everyone out of the house immediately. I'm coming home."

Now the panic was starting to burn at the back of my throat. What was going on? "Just please tell me you're all right," I begged. "Please, I need to know!"

"I'm fine. I just need you to get everyone out of the house."

"How long is it going to take you to get home?"

"I'll be home in twenty minutes."

"Mark, I can't wait twenty minutes! You need to tell me what's going on!"

His next words came out in a rush. "It's my father. My father has done something very bad, and is probably going to jail for the rest of his life."

We hung up, and I felt relief flood through me. I had been so scared that something had happened to Mark that I didn't even wonder what Bernie had done. As long as Mark was okay, nothing else mattered in that moment. Now I had to get the others out of the house.

I tried to compose myself, but Susan took one look at my face and saw how upset I was.

"Stephanie, what's wrong? Are you okay?"

The lie came to me quickly, without thought.

"I'm really sorry, guys," I said. "I have to go. That was just my ob-gyn. I got bad results on a glucose test and he needs to repeat it because I might have gestational diabetes." Mere mention of the ob-gyn had the contractor packing up and bustling out the door, but Susan stayed put. I felt instantly guilty about the worried expression on her face.

"Let me drive you up there," she offered.

"No, no, no," I insisted. "It's okay, I'll just jump in a cab."

She left, reluctantly, and I waited anxiously for the sound of the elevator coming back up, silently urging Mark to hurry home. When he finally walked through the door, it was hard to believe he was the same man who had been breezily discussing baby names and laughing over stupid love songs a couple of hours earlier. His face was ashen, his body almost electric with anger. I followed him into our bedroom and shut the door. We sat on the bed, and he put his head in his hands.

"I've spoken to Marty already, but I wanted to come home and tell you in person," he began. My stepfather was retired at that point, but had been a partner at one of the city's premier law firms. "I only have a few minutes, then I have to go meet with attorneys and the authorities," Mark went on. "My father did something bad—what he did is probably going to crash the stock market."

These staccato pieces of information weren't fitting together. I made him stop and go back over the morning from the beginning.

Bernie had called his sons into his office and told them to prepare their proposals for employee bonuses; he was going to distribute them early this year. Mark and Andy had immediately been suspicious; that never happened, and it made no sense. Bonuses were based on year-end performances. Traditionally, Wall Street bonuses are doled out in January or February, and Madoff Securities had always paid theirs out on the later side. Mark and Andy objected to the unexpected switch and wanted to know why Bernie was changing the timing now. Bernie remained adamant, but offered no real explanation. He looked haggard. Mark left the meeting thinking his worst hunch was proving true: His father was terminally ill. The two brothers had retreated, then regrouped and decided to confront their father again. They had marched back into Bernie's office. Mark took the lead.

"What the fuck is going on?" he demanded.

"I can't tell you here," Bernie replied. "We need to leave. Let's go to my apartment." The penthouse where Ruth and Bernie lived, at East 64th Street just off Lexington Avenue, was a few blocks away. On the way out, they made excuses to the secretaries about going gift shopping so the sight of all three Madoffs suddenly leaving together in the middle of the morning wouldn't set the employee rumor mill churning.

At the apartment, Mark and Andy found their mother sitting on the living room couch, her face completely devoid of expression, looking as if she were in an open-eyed coma. She sat there wordlessly. Bernie spoke.

"It's all one big lie," he told his sons. His elite investment advisory business, with its private fund that Bernie personally managed and billionaires begged to join, was nothing but an enormous, international Ponzi scheme. There were no investments, no brilliant returns, just somewhere around $50 billion in debts that he couldn't pay. Bernie betrayed no emotion or remorse, calmly delivering his bombshell with the cool demeanor of an anchorman reading a wire report on the evening news. When he was done, he began to cry. He said he would be distributing approximately $140 million in "bonuses" to family and friends, then consulting his attorney about turning himself in a week later. He would probably go to jail, he added pointlessly. Ruth, a woman who never had nothing to say, remained silent and zombielike. The two elder Madoffs watched blankly as their sons tried to absorb the unfathomable betrayal. Andy crumpled to the floor, sobbing. Mark was shaking with rage. He tugged at his brother to get up.

"Let's get the fuck out of here!" Mark said.

The brothers stormed out. Neither parent made a move to follow.

Out on the street, Mark immediately dialed my stepfather's number. Marty heard the tension in his son-in-law's voice. He and Andy needed to see him; could they come right over? Marty gave him the room number of the hotel where he and my mother were camping out while closing the sale of their apartment. When Marty opened the door, he could see that Mark and Andy were both obviously distraught, pale and shaking. They repeated what Bernie had told them.

Marty debriefed Mark and Andy for a couple of hours, trying to piece together what was happening, then began assembling a legal team for them both, turning to the top experts in his old law firm. Mark and Andy had made up their minds the minute they had fled their parents' penthouse.

They were turning their father in.

It was a decision that should have made them heroes, but would instead, for the foreseeable future, cost them everything—their family, their livelihoods, and their own good reputations. Exposing their father would bring them under scrutiny as well, even though neither Mark nor Andy had worked for the fraudulent fund. But the Ponzi scheme Bernie had run for decades would turn out to be the biggest in history, and those closest to him were inevitably caught in its cold shadow, regardless of their innocence.

Mark spent the rest of that grueling day in a series of intense meetings with his lawyers and in phone consultations with federal authorities. Back home, I paced the polished floors. All I could do was wait and worry, assured only by the terse little text messages that popped up on my phone every hour or so from my husband: *Still meeting.* I tried to keep calm for the sake of the baby I was carrying; I couldn't afford to stress out and put him at risk. I just wanted Mark to come home. What was happening? What did it all mean? What had Bernie done? The office party was that night—were we supposed to go and load up our plates at the taco bar and pretend nothing was wrong?

It was late at night by the time Mark appeared, ragged and spent. He had contacted the Securities and Exchange Commission and the

U.S. Attorney's Office and told the appropriate authorities that his father, the King Midas of Wall Street, the great, vaunted Bernie Madoff, was a fraud. A con man. A phony. A criminal. They had no proof, no documents, no inside knowledge. All they had was their father's confession. Mark and Andy were scheduled to be at their lawyers' offices the next morning to meet with investigators from the U.S. Attorney's Office and SEC officials.

That evening, our unanswered phones were filled with text messages and voice mails from friends at the firm, partying at the Mexican restaurant. *Hey, where r u guys?* Ruth and Bernie were there, everyone was having a great time, what was keeping the Madoff brothers? The staff had no idea what horror would face them in the morning, when a swarm of federal agents would descend on their offices with search warrants.

Mark was lying prone on our bed, crying. I had never seen someone I loved so hurt, so deeply anguished. My attempts to comfort him felt small and useless. I could tell he was exhausted and in shock, his emotions careening from fear to disbelief to anger to despair. What if his father killed himself, and he and Andy were blamed for the Ponzi scheme? What was going to happen to his mother? Mark couldn't believe that Bernie's confession in the penthouse that morning was the first time Ruth was hearing the awful news; she had been too calm, so disturbingly emotionless that it crossed Mark's mind that she might have been medicated. That in itself was telling. Ruth wasn't one of those *Valley of the Dolls* socialites; a bottle of wine was her usual poison. Mark didn't know what he was supposed to think of either parent anymore. His pain was almost palpable. Had his whole life been built on his father's lies? What kind of monster was the man he idolized?

I held him in the dark, twining myself around his arm and putting my head on his shoulder. I was scared, too.

"What's going to happen next?" I whispered.

Mark's voice, scraped raw from grief, sounded small and far away.

"I don't know."

two

Big Fish

He knew by the third date; I knew on the fourth.

I've always believed in soul mates. I grew up feeling absolutely certain that there was someone out there in the world meant only for me, and I assumed that we would eventually find each other and spend our lives together, because it was just meant to be that way. I took it on faith. It's not as if I were one of those daydreamy little girls who played bride in her bedroom with a half-slip veil on her head and a bouquet of Kleenex carnations in her hands. I was more of a tomboy. But at heart, yes, I was a pure romantic.

By the time my twenty-seventh birthday rolled around and I was still single, however, I was beginning to lose patience with fate. What was taking so long? Most of my friends who weren't married were at least in relationships that were headed that way. Given the disastrous choices I'd made so far on the boyfriend front, my personal GPS needed some serious reprogramming if a lifetime commitment was the destination. So, as much as I'd like to claim that it was Cinderella optimism that made me agree to a blind date one bleary morning at the gym, it was probably just mounting panic. I figured I didn't have much more time to waste if I wanted that happily-ever-after family I'd always imagined.

"Listen," said my locker-room matchmaker, a woman who was barely a nodding acquaintance from our respective weight machines, "I'm not going to guarantee anything, but I will tell you I met my husband on a blind date." She was on a mission to pay it forward, apparently. Her eligible friend, she went on, was a thirty-seven-year-old guy named Mark Madoff, divorced with two kids, and he was probably one of the wealthiest men in New York City. My mind immediately seized on what I considered the one relevant detail:

Thirty-seven years old? Ewww.

That was an entire decade gaping between us. He would have been graduating from college when I was still in grade school! He would want to hit the early-bird smorgasbord when I wanted to go clubbing. Never mind that I didn't actually go clubbing—I might want to when I was sixty-two, and I didn't want my salsa partner to be using a walker. My mom's voice interrupted my inner monologue before I could go much further: "Take any date you can get, Stephanie." Mom had a point, but she was also probably even more anxious than I was. She and my stepfather worried that I was on my way to becoming the spinster daughter they would have to help support forever while she flitted from one artsy job to the next, always ridiculously overqualified and even more ridiculously underpaid.

At the time, I was the assistant to designer Narciso Rodriguez, a position that, had we been cartoon characters, would have made me his loyal Chihuahua sidekick. My duties encompassed everything from booking his trips to Europe and making dinner reservations at the hottest restaurants to stopping at Bloomingdale's to buy his favorite underwear. I also got to sit in on shoe-design meetings and loan my feet for inspiration—they were perfect shoe-model size 7½.

It was exciting to be part of such a hot young designer's team, but the job wasn't doing a thing for my bank account or my social life. As much as I loved being in the fashion industry, Seventh Avenue isn't exactly a meet market for straight women. I knew more men dying to dress me for a date than take me on one, and the droughts were starting to last longer and longer. My mother helpfully pointed out that the pool of eligible men my age was quickly evaporating. I considered the alternative, picturing myself sitting alone with too many spider plants in some basement apartment, watching feet constantly scurry past on the sidewalk outside my iron-grated window.

Maybe a divorced daddy pushing forty wasn't out of the question after all.

Of course, I did due Google-diligence first, researching "Mark Madoff" until I found some photos. Not trusting my own instant attraction—athletic, full head of brown hair, hazel eyes, warm smile— I sought validating opinions from all the gay men at work. They unanimously agreed: Mark was handsome. (This straw poll made perfect sense at the time.)

Our first date was at a French bistro called Casimir in the East Village, then a slowly gentrifying neighborhood in what once was a dangerous maze of high-rise projects. Mark later admitted that he had picked a place downtown, far from both of our Upper East Side apartments, as a bit of a test: He wanted someone with a sense of adventure, not some high-maintenance Park Avenue princess. Little did he know that my office was actually a few blocks from the restaurant. I considered myself a downtown girl through and through, despite—or maybe because of—the privileged world I'd grown up around.

That night, I raced uptown after work to shower and change into black pants and a simple but sexy black sleeveless top Narciso had given me. Then I headed back downtown for the big date. Mark was sitting at the bar drinking a bottle of Stella Artois when I walked in, and we immediately fell into the kind of comfortable conversation that feels like it's resuming, not just beginning, as if we were just pulling through a thread that had stitched our lives together long ago. He started talking about a fishing trip he'd just been on.

"I pretty much grew up fishing," I volunteered.

"Oh?" He sounded dubious. "What kind?"

"I've caught bluefish, and I've been tuna and shark fishing," I boasted. "My parents would drug us with Dramamine and take us four hours out into the Atlantic."

Mark was unimpressed. He was a fly-fisherman himself. I had no idea then that there was a caste system in the fishing world and I had just revealed myself to be one of the untouchables. I prattled on, happily recounting how we used to dump canned corn over the side of the boat to lure flounder.

"That's cheating!" Mark needled. As if tying handcrafted fake flies on your fishing hook wasn't. I still thought my tuna trumped his trout.

The date flew by pleasantly, and after dinner we shared a cab uptown. Our apartments turned out to be only a few blocks apart. "Thanks, I had a great time," Mark said as he dropped me off with a gentlemanly hug. My mom called as soon as I was in the elevator, her radar still as keen as it had been back when I was a teenager sneaking home after curfew.

"How'd it go?" she wanted to know.

"Mom, he is the *nicest* guy," I gushed. "And he loves to fish!"

"That's great! He must have been impressed that you've caught tuna and shark." She sounded pleased; maybe letting small children help you chum for six-foot mako sharks off the back of a boat wasn't such a parenting faux pas after all.

"Not really," I admitted.

"Did he say he wanted to go out again?" Mom demanded.

"No."

"Well, that's ridiculous, Stephanie. If he had a great time, why not say he was going to call, or ask you out again? He doesn't know what he's missing!" He hadn't even met her, but Mark had already pissed off my mother. I realized that I should probably be upset, too, but I couldn't decide whether to be mad at Mom for deflating me post-date, at Mark for leaving me hanging, or at both, just on principle. I went to bed confused.

The next day, our matchmaker reported back that Mark thought I was definitely worth a second date, and soon enough, Mark himself called. He wanted me to know that he would be tied up for the next three weeks between business and a spring break trip with his kids, but he wanted to get together when he returned. I was back on cloud nine. When I hit the gym as usual at six a.m. the following morning, I felt entitled to dismiss the two guys checking me out from their recumbent bikes. *Oh, c'mon,* I thought, *are you really ogling me at this hour?* I jumped on the treadmill and started my daily run, listening to music and watching the *Today* show on the television mounted in front of me. I was in my zone when one of the oglers sidled up to my treadmill. Annoyed, I refused to acknowledge him. He refused to take the hint.

"Uh, Stephanie?" I heard him ask. I turned to look at him, startled that he knew my name. "We had a date two days ago and actually we made another one."

Mark.

He never would confess that he'd intentionally come to check me out with his buddy, but I'd been going to that gym at six a.m. religiously for over five years, and it was deserted enough at that hour to recognize the regulars, and I knew he wasn't one of them. I guess I passed the how-does-she-look-sweaty-and-half-asleep-with-no-makeup test, because he didn't stand me up for our second date. That one was at a Mexican restaurant. Years later, he would remember that our dishes got mixed up and I ate his striped bass instead of my own salmon—already fish was a recurring theme for us—and I would remember only that I spent the evening thinking how much he looked like Kevin Costner. He walked me home, and when we reached my apartment building, we perched on the ledge at the bottom of the steps, not wanting to say good-bye. I prayed he wouldn't try to kiss me while the doorman was watching, and offered my cheek when he moved in to say good night.

Mark's wealth wasn't something we discussed, and he never flaunted it. My own family was comfortable, but by no means in the same league as some of my classmates at the private Nightingale-Bamford School on East 92nd Street. I wasn't a Waldorf-Astoria debutante in a Vera Wang gown. My stepfather, Marty London, was a litigator and partner in a firm with an impressive roster of clients, though we didn't live a lavish lifestyle. Unlike other tenth-graders I knew in high school, I couldn't stroll into a trendy boutique and casually snap up a $1,200 handbag because it was cute, nor could I buy all the makeup and Betsey Johnson clothes I wanted on a credit card with no limit. I didn't have a credit card. My allowance was meant to cover burgers and a movie on the weekend. We were well-off, but I never shared the Junior League aspirations of some of my wealthier peers. What was the point? The social registry didn't list the biggest fish you ever caught.

At Nightingale, I fell into a tight-knit clique of five girls. We called ourselves the Breakfast Club after the John Hughes movie, because our personalities matched those of the main characters. We also bought fake IDs off some Trinity guys who ran a booming business selling them to the prep-school crowd that partied in the clubs and bars along First, Second, and Third avenues on the Upper East Side. The phony IDs were so easy to pass off that no one ever even questioned why mine had an M for gender instead of an F.

One of our favorite spots senior year was Dorrian's, which had gained notoriety in the 1986 "preppy murder" case. At Drake's Drum, we ordered frozen Mudslides and shots of Jägermeister, which makes me nauseated now even to recall. We thought we were terribly sophisticated. I made good grades and rarely got caught breaking my eleven thirty curfew (or sneaking back out after my parents were asleep). I even had a clever system to circumvent the rules when my folks were out of town. They would leave the doorman a list of friends—girls only—who could be allowed up when they were gone. I would just have the boys buzz a friend who lived five floors above us, and she would let them in; they would take the elevator up to twelve and walk down the back stairwell to my apartment on seven, where the party was under way.

By the time I met Mark, my wild days were long over, and I had no desire to relive them. I'd given up smoking, taken up running, and considered a second glass of white wine a party. We both preferred quiet evenings at neighborhood restaurants or watching TV with takeout from our favorite sushi joint.

Our third date was spontaneous. Mark called after I'd gotten out of the shower at nine o'clock one night to see if I wanted to meet for a drink in our neighborhood. I showed up with my damp hair in a ponytail and my Timex watch accessorizing jeans, a T-shirt, and sneakers. He told me I looked great, and later confided that he knew at that moment that he was falling in love.

For me, the real turning point was our fourth date. "I don't know if you're interested," Mark said. "It may be a pain in the neck, but I have a black-tie business event to go to." It was the annual Security Traders Association ball. Mark was worried that I would have to get a formal dress just for his occasion. I had no such worries: Narciso to the rescue, again. When I told the guys at work about the invitation, everyone dropped what they were doing to dress me. Narciso loaned me a black sleeveless crepe de chine gown with a sexy, open back.

"What about shoes?" I asked my coworker and de facto stylist, Simon, who has the best taste of anyone I've ever met. Simon instructed me to go out and buy a pair of Christian Louboutin evening sandals, which he described in precise detail. They cost me half my paycheck; I'd never dropped so much on a pair of shoes in my life. Clearly I was getting serious. Simon then gave me a tutorial on how to properly tie the satin ribbon around my ankle—one loop, to the side. I wore simple diamond stud earrings made from my grandmother's wedding ring.

When the big night arrived, I ended up missing the whole cocktail hour because I had to work. Mark sent a Madoff driver named Clive to pick me up in one of the firm's black BMWs and whisk me to the Hilton Hotel on Sixth Avenue, and I arrived just as dinner was about to begin. I nearly fainted at the sight of Mark in a tux, he looked so gorgeous. Next thing I knew, Mark was called up to the microphone to make a speech. I'd had no idea he was the STANY president. Flushed with pride, he kissed me when he sat back down. It was our first kiss.

After that night, we were just together. Fate, I was certain, had finally come through. Cupid, on the other hand, would need a little coaching: The first time Mark sent me flowers, he signed the little card "From: Mark Madoff."

As clueless as I was about Mark's status in the financial world, I was vaguely aware of his father's high profile. Bernard Madoff was King Midas, and the media lapped up the colorful story of a plumber's son from Queens going from penny stockbroker to billionaire. Bernie had served as non-executive chairman of NASDAQ and was often sought out by the media as an expert to quote on the market. I wasn't familiar with any of these details, but had an old friend who worked on Wall Street and who suddenly couldn't stop bragging about the guy her friend was seeing. A few months after Mark and I became a couple, I finally met the famous Bernie Madoff in person.

"Hey, my parents are having lunch at Craftbar. Let's go join them," Mark suggested one weekend morning. I instantly freaked out: He couldn't just casually spring this on me! Meeting the parents is a big deal in a relationship. You don't just nonchalantly saunter over to lunch. What was he thinking? There wasn't time to argue or make excuses to back out, though, which was obviously Mark's plan all along in an attempt to keep it low-key. He hadn't officially met my parents yet, though he had run into my mom when I was moving into a new apartment and he dropped by with some scented candles—he loved candles—and other little housewarming gifts. There was a certain protocol to these things in my mind, and he was blithely ignoring all the rules.

At the restaurant, my anxiety was immediately put to rest: Ruth and Bernie proved to be down-to-earth and charming. I liked them both instantly. Bernie was quiet, but not in an aloof or distracted way. There was something very sweet about him. Ruth, on the other hand, was clearly the live wire in the relationship. Petite, with a once elfin prettiness that had been artfully maintained, Mark's mother was a born performer who commanded attention. She was quick-witted and completely unfiltered, and her one-liners and hilarious stories kept me in stitches the whole time.

As often as not, I would come to learn, Ruth's funniest anecdotes were at her bemused husband's expense. One of their classics was about the time the Madoffs had been invited to spend a couple of days aboard *Kisses*, the magnificent yacht of billionaire friends in the Caribbean. It was so elegant, there were original Picassos hanging on the walls. When Bernie woke up on board the first morning, he was horrified to see dark streaks on his bed linens, and he shamefully assumed he had soiled himself while he slept. That night, Ruth noticed the Hershey's Kisses left on their bed by the crew at turndown; it was melted chocolate Bernie had been rolling around in the night before. Bernie laughed, too, when she retold the story.

I thought Mark was incredibly lucky to have such great parents, and as a child of divorce, I deeply admired their marriage of forty-plus years. Bernie and Ruth had been high school sweethearts, and still went to the movies together almost every single day after work. It was their little ritual, and they would watch anything from *School of Rock* to the latest indie art flick about the Holocaust. The only rule was that it had to be playing in a theater where Bernie could get a signal for his cell phone so he could stay in touch with clients and his seventeenth-floor staff at the Lipstick Building. He refused to go anywhere, either during a routine day or outside of the country on vacation, where he might not get phone service.

Ruth seemed totally unperturbed by her husband's overwhelming success and his celebrity; she was confident enough of her place in his life that she could remain blasé about Bernie making their Thai house-keeper give him massages on his home massage table. Both Bernie and Ruth infuriate me now, but honestly, when I looked at the two of them back then, I hoped to have the same kind of marriage someday with their son.

Mark was always considered the more gregarious of the two Madoff boys. Andy, younger by two years, was more intense and re-served. Despite their very different personalities, the brothers had always been close to each other, and their friendship had deepened in adulthood as each went through the turmoil of a failed marriage and the challenges of being a single father. The dominant relationship in Mark's life was beyond a doubt that with his two children. When I met Mark, I was young and naïve enough to believe that goodwill was all I would need to forge a loving relationship with Kate and Daniel. Mark's divorce was so far behind him—years at that point—that I assumed all the emotional dust with his ex had long since settled. It wouldn't take long to discover how very wrong I was.

When we began dating, Mark was usually out of the office and on the road to his house in Greenwich by three o'clock on Friday afternoons. I was happy enough to reconnect with my own circle of friends on the weekend; it was refreshing not to fall into that age-old trap of ignoring your girlfriends because there's a new man in your life. Kate and Daniel were Mark's greatest source of pride, and being a father was so much a part of his identity that my shorthand for him when dissecting the relationship with my girlfriends was simply "the dad."

Naturally, I was eager to meet Mark's kids, but he wanted to go slowly on that front. He had dated plenty of women after becoming single again, but his last serious relationship since the divorce had been pretty volatile, and he wasn't going to thrust his kids into the middle of anything until he felt certain it was safe. His caution was understandable, but it could be maddening, especially to someone as young as I was; I had no clue yet what it was like to be a parent, much less how agonizing it is to be separated from the children you adore and how tentative that can make you. Inserting me into their cozy equation was not something Mark was in any hurry to do. I felt my resentment building over what I took to be my own unworthiness.

The ultimate insult came the first summer of our romance, when Mark pointedly didn't invite me to the famed Madoff company beach party in Montauk because Kate was going to be there and the kids still hadn't met me (her brother was at sleepaway camp). I felt dismissed, but I swallowed the hurt and didn't say anything; I was too afraid Mark might dump me if I were anything less than pleasant and agreeable, and I was falling for him hard. Mark hated confrontation, and I knew already that he would do anything to avoid it.

While the big beach bash was getting under way, I spent that Friday by myself at the radiologist, having an MRI done on my hip. What had started out as an ache I attributed to my daily workout had turned into such searing pain I could barely walk.

"Stephanie, you've got to see a doctor," Mark had urged me. "My good friend owns the Mets. Do you mind if I call him for a recommendation?" So there I was, a treadmill casualty in the offices of one of the country's top sports doctors. I limped home and spent the weekend nursing both my bum hip and my bruised ego. On Monday morning, the doctor rang my cell phone.

"Where are you?" The controlled urgency in his voice sent a ripple of fear down my spine.

"On my way to work—why?"

"Get in a cab and come to my office right now, and don't hit any potholes on the way," he ordered me. The MRI had revealed a stress fracture, and my right hip was on the verge of a full-blown break. I would have to take it easy and spend the next two months on crutches.

Mark was solicitous, but staying home was out of the question when he produced tickets to an acoustic Counting Crows concert that weekend at a small Lower East Side club. A buddy from Mark's office and his wife joined us. They spent much of the evening reminiscing about how great the Montauk party had been the weekend before; the wife couldn't stop gushing about how fabulous everything was. The big barbecue on the beach, the lobster bake under the stars, the Good Humor truck that had been rented, fully stocked, for all the children to enjoy. Mark seemed oblivious to how hurtful and rude the conversation was to me. I feigned interest, then went home and cried. I wanted to be a part of this man's life, not excluded from it.

When their mother took the kids on a Disney cruise over Christmas break that December, Mark and I slipped away for our first real vacation together, to Little Palm Island, a resort and spa in the Florida Keys. On our way, we stopped to spend a night with Ruth and Bernie at their home in Palm Beach. In New York, we tended to see Mark's parents at events or in restaurants. In Florida, being with them for those twenty-four hours in their home environment would give me an ugly glimpse into a side of them I had never seen before.

The two of them spent the entire time trash-talking the help. Ruth barked commands at the housekeeper, Marlena, and mocked her Spanish accent. Bernie was fastidiously neat to the point of being obsessive-compulsive, and, with Ruth, he complained ad nauseam about the maid's incompetence. Even worse, Captain Dick, the man who looked after Bernie's boats, kept coming in to use the toilet, which Bernie would then inspect. The rest of us were then treated to his crude description of what he had seen, and his almost girlish outrage over how disgusted he was, as he launched into yet another rant about how "useless" Marlena was. I couldn't wait to get out of there.

Little Palm Island, on the other hand, was pure paradise. It was as if we had stepped back in time into the scene of some epic,

Hemingwayesque romance. Thatched open-air bungalows perched on stilts above crystal blue waters, and the grounds were lush with tropical flowers and vines. Our canopy bed was draped in gauzy mosquito netting that softly billowed in the breeze. It felt like a honeymoon. Excitedly exploring our suite, I discovered that the guest amenities included personalized stationery waiting on the desktop. MR. AND MRS. MADOFF, it elegantly proclaimed. I quickly threw it away so Mark wouldn't see it. No point spooking him.

We took a boat out deep-sea fishing, and I was excited when Mark hooked a big one. Our guide identified it as a grouper and wanted to cut the line—groupers are enormous and a pain to haul in. The big ones don't taste all that great, and they're endangered to boot. "No, you gotta reel it in!" I urged Mark. Machismo won out, and he fought the hundred-pound fish to the finish. I was duly impressed.

I had already established my sportsmanship on an earlier weekend getaway to Key West, where we went out on a flats-fishing boat one day in hopes of catching a prized permit or tarpon in the shallow waters. We had barely gotten under way when a big wake came along and swamped the boat, completely soaking us both. There was a moment of shocked silence. Then I turned to Mark and we both started laughing hysterically. When I looked down, there was a little needle-nose fish in the boat. It would be the only one we caught that day.

We'd been together eleven months before Mark finally introduced me to his children. Kate and Daniel had come to the city on one of their weekends with their dad, and Mark decided it was time for them to meet his "friend." I brought them cupcakes, and we all went to a paint-your-own-pottery shop, then out to see a kiddie movie called *The Wild Thornberrys*. Kate was seven years old, and Daniel was ten. I thought they were cute, sweet kids, and Mark happily reported back that they liked me, too. I felt as if I had passed the bar exam. Now we could be a real couple!

That illusion was quickly shattered when Mark asked me to come along on a weekend visit with the kids in Greenwich, only to insist that I sleep in the maid's room. "This is how the child psychologist said we should do it," Mark insisted. When Kate's cousins and little friends came over to play, they assumed I was the new nanny.

Becoming a part of Mark's time with his kids came with the unwanted bonus of a new social director in my life: Mark's ex. Susan called incessantly during his visitation time, wanting to speak to the kids or to Mark, peppering him with unsolicited advice about what activities he might do with Kate and Daniel, what to feed them, where to take them shopping, and so on. I wondered why he put up with it. "She's their mother," he would say defensively. It was easier to indulge her than to cross her. I wasn't quite as willing to be bulldozed, and her meddling soon ignited our first big fight.

It was Labor Day weekend, and Mark and I had taken the kids with us to spend the holiday at the beach with Bernie and Ruth at their house in Montauk. As it turned out, two other families Mark and the kids knew from Greenwich had rented a place a couple of miles down the road. Susan called and instructed Mark to take the kids to spend the day with their friends. I tried to object. This was his time with Kate and Daniel, and their grandparents didn't deserve to be treated as a mere staging ground. Besides, I would feel awkward hanging out on the beach with people who had been friends of Mark and Susan's when they were together; on the other hand, sending Mark alone would seem rude and petty. Mark, as usual, ended up ceding to his ex's demands, and off we went. Sure enough, the Greenwich wives spent the afternoon interrogating me. Where did I get my hair colored? What exactly did I do for Narciso Rodriguez?

"Is that T-shirt a Narciso Rodriguez?" one of the husbands even asked.

"Um, no, it's from the Gap," I replied, wondering who on earth would wear a $300 designer T-shirt on the beach. With a pair of comfy old cutoffs, no less.

I was being sized up, and I knew a full report would be dished back to Mark's ex-wife. Later that day, when Mark and I went into town to run errands without the kids, I vented my frustration.

"Why did you let her do that to us?" I demanded. "This is *our* weekend with *your* children. Why does she have to have a say in whatever we do?"

"Well," Mark sputtered, "I thought it would be fun for the kids to be with their friends."

"They see each other in Greenwich all the time!" I was yelling by now. Why did he have to be such a wimp when it came to his ex-wife? Didn't he see that this wasn't about a playdate? It was about control, and he needed to stand up for himself and assert his right to enjoy his visitation time free from their mother's interference, which was so constant that it felt like borderline stalking.

We got past the tension between us by ignoring it until it dissipated. I told myself to just suck it up, which wouldn't be the last time I made that same mistake. The feeling that I came third in Mark's life—after his children, which was to be expected, and after his ex, which was not—would become so entrenched that it would drive us eventually to couple's therapy. Nothing ever really changed, though. We were always trying to shoot those rapids, and we never fully succeeded. It just became a matter of how emotionally bruised and battered we'd get in the process.

Not long after my Montauk outburst, Mark broached the subject of moving in together. We had been seeing each other for about a year and a half. I had just moved into an apartment in my dream building on a quiet stretch of East 63rd Street—a tiny alcove studio with plenty of sunshine—but I was hardly ever around to enjoy it, since I spent every night at Mark's. When Mark casually asked if I wanted to keep some clothes at his place, the discussion segued into whether we should live together. I was thrilled that he had brought it up and that he felt committed enough to take our relationship to the next level, too.

I sold all my college-era furniture and kitchen stuff to my doorman, and came with little more than my clothes and my Twelve Days of Christmas plates. Mark's place, though larger, was a classic bachelor pad, and I sensed he was nervous about the impending invasion of two X chromosomes. One day, I went to the drugstore and bought tons of feminine products—tampons, douches, anything I could think of. I snuck into the bathroom and stuffed his medicine cabinet to the bursting point, so it would all come tumbling out on him when he went to shave in the morning. My wicked attempt at aversion therapy cracked him up and made me love him even more for being able to laugh at himself.

My heart just felt light around him, buoyant. We took genuine delight in each other's company, and, save for the Labor Day quarrel, we had never fought about anything else. I was determined to be the perfect girlfriend, a sweet, understanding, good-sport partner who needed nothing more than to love and be loved by him. Mark was a lot more experienced and battle-scarred than I was, though, and he must have seen through the act pretty easily. A few months after I'd moved in, we were out at dinner when, out of the blue, before our appetizers had even arrived, he suddenly announced, "You need to know that I'm really soured on the idea of marriage."

I was speechless, then furious. I swiped away the tears streaming down my face. "You've ruined everything," I told him.

A pair of older women who'd been having dinner at the next table were getting ready to go, and one of them chose that moment to lean across and say something. "You know, you two make an adorable couple!" she trilled, oblivious to the drama she had just interrupted. Mark excused himself and got up to go to the men's room. I sat there fuming. Why had he asked me to move in, let me give up my own apartment? I was twenty-nine. I'd never been married, I didn't have children of my own yet. What gave him the right to presume I didn't want all that?

"Let's just go," I said when he returned to the table. I yelled at him the whole way home. "Why did you bring that up?" I demanded. "I *never* bring up marriage with you!"

"I just think it's important you know my views," Mark responded. To him, it was a matter of integrity—one of the very qualities that I admired most in him—but to me, it was a matter of timing, and his stunk.

I spent the next few weeks in a quiet state of panic. *What am I going to do?* I asked myself virtually every waking moment. I was too humiliated to confide in my parents or any of my friends, or ask for advice. Finally, I decided to just go with my gut. I didn't want to break up. I couldn't imagine life without him, without loving him. I was going to stay. I'd be able to change his mind, I convinced myself.

We pretended nothing had happened, and the subject didn't come up again until nearly a year later, on my thirtieth birthday. We were planning a big party in two weeks to celebrate the milestone with seventy-five friends. Things were going really well. Mark had bought a new apartment in SoHo, and we had just moved in. Downtown was our natural habitat, and we loved our neighborhood with its eclectic mix of shopping, restaurants, artsy street vendors, and colorful people. This truly felt like *our* home, rather than me merely inhabiting his. We were still waiting for the furniture we'd ordered to arrive, and the only things in our living room were four beanbag chairs, a table, and a heavy desk lamp. Looking around one morning while getting ready to leave for work, I suddenly flipped out, realizing that I had given up my own little dream apartment to move in with him, but here I was, almost thirty years old, playing house with no promise.

"I cannot be the girlfriend anymore!" I shrieked. Mark looked up, dumbfounded, from his beanbag. "I need more!" I went on. "I just can't take it anymore!" With that, I picked the lamp up off the table and threw it on the floor, leaving a dent in the polished wood. I stomped out the door. I spent the day distracted and going through the motions at work. *This sucks, but I can't wait anymore*, I told myself. I knew Mark would break up with me, but so be it. If he couldn't commit, I needed to move on. Reaching our door after work, I was scared to go inside.

In the living room, Mark was back in the same beanbag he'd been in that morning. He stood up, and wordlessly walked over to hug me.

"I don't have a ring yet. I'd been planning on asking you at your birthday party, in front of all our friends and family," he said. He got down on his knee anyway and asked me to be his wife.

My birthday party turned into an engagement party. I felt like an idiot. A very happy one.

I had always wanted a destination wedding, and St. Barths, where my parents had a vacation home, was my top pick. But once I started planning my wedding, I realized that a lot of my friends wouldn't be able to afford to go if I tied the knot with Mark in some faraway resort. We decided on Nantucket instead. It was where we had spent our very first weekend away together, and we both loved its quaint cobblestoned streets and breathtaking shoreline. Nantucket touched someplace deep in Mark's fisherman soul, and he even loved the overpoweringly sharp, briny smell of the beach at low tide. We reserved the weekend of October 23, 2004, at the elegant White Elephant Hotel overlooking Nantucket Harbor.

Since she'd never had any daughters, I invited Ruth to help my mom and me plan the wedding. She added to the fun and never overstepped her boundaries. I thought she was going to make the ideal mother-in-law, if there could be such a thing. My mother liked her, too.

My tastes run to chic but simple, and the bottom line was that everyone had to be comfortable and have a good time at the wedding. I wanted it to be laid-back, not stiff and formal. I didn't want to be dressed like a big cupcake bride. I did have one extravagance in mind, though. "I don't care if I have to wear a paper bag and carry a single flower," I told the event planners at our first meeting. "I want the Harlem Boys Choir to perform."

Narciso was designing my gown as a wedding gift, and I didn't have any say in what it would look like. What might have been terrifying for your average bridezilla was thrilling to me; I knew he would create something special and uniquely my own. I didn't want a veil, and would have gone with a simple ponytail, but my hairdresser convinced me to at least let him twist it into an effortless knot. A friend who designed jewelry made me one of the island's signature rope bracelets, intertwining thin strands of white gold. Mark chose a gray suit with a blue-checked shirt and a gold tie emblazoned with tiny fish. Kate and Daniel would escort their father down the aisle of the wedding tent on a carpet with orange rose petals, and I would make my entrance to the sweet, soaring voices of the Boys Choir of Harlem. We'd submitted a list of twenty-five songs, and the choir had chosen three. Ruth had stepped in at the last minute and nixed a gospel tune on the grounds that it had the words "Jesus Christ" in the lyrics. I was surprised by her decree, since the Madoffs weren't observant Jews, but it was no big deal to change songs if it placated her.

The ceremony was casual, presided over by an old friend of my family, former New York prosecutor-turned-novelist Linda Fairstein, who was warm and ebullient. At the reception afterward, the hundred or so guests sat down to a Thanksgiving dinner. Granted, it was a month early, but it had always been my favorite holiday meal, and it was an autumn wedding, so why not serve roast turkey with stuffing and all the trimmings?

I was deliriously happy, dancing all night in an exquisite backless Narciso sheath. Mark kept drifting in and out of my reach. Daniel was acting out, competing for his father's attention by poking him with straws, and Mark had to tend to him for much of the reception. The adults were cranked up, too. In addition to the carrot wedding cake, there was a dessert bar overflowing with Twinkies, Sno Balls, Snickers bars, and Starburst candies. Eight years later, people still tell me it was the best wedding ever. It probably took a good five years just for the sugar high to wear off.

My new father-in-law, a teetotaler, watched much of the gaiety from his preferred seat on the sidelines. When I catch a glimpse of him on our wedding video, it's impossible to read the half smile on his face. I took it then for happiness, but like everything else about Bernie now, I don't know what was real. He and I had gotten into a huge fight the day after Mark had put a gorgeous engagement ring on my finger. Mark had come home from the office that night looking uncomfortable.

"We need to discuss something you may not be happy about," he told me. "You're going to have to sign a prenup. It's more to protect my dad's business." Bernie, he explained, was insisting on it.

My hackles rose instantly. "What does he think I am, some kind of a gold digger? Nice." Ruth had come over to congratulate me in person the morning after Mark proposed, while Bernie apparently was busy having his lawyers draw up a document that anticipated our divorce. He had rendered the most beautiful moment of my life so far into something cold and calculating. Feeling spiteful, I flat-out refused to sign. Did Mark and his parents really have such doubts about my character? When I told my parents what was happening, I was surprised to hear my stepdad take Bernie's side.

"You know what, Steph, I don't blame him," Marty said. "He's worked hard to build his business, and you're not entitled to his hundreds and hundreds of millions."

I was still upset. I didn't care about diamonds or dollars. This was about trust, and simple respect, qualities that I thought needed to be obvious for any marriage to succeed, regardless of either party's respective bank account. I felt accused and insulted. Mark left me to stew while he went on a two-day fishing trip with his brother, who had had a rough year fighting cancer and dealing with his own marital crisis. Bernie called and left me a message, and I ducked outside my office at Narciso's to call him back from the street, ready for a showdown. I was hurt and offended, and I wanted him to know it.

"You didn't make Susan sign one, or Debbie," I protested. If Mark's and Andy's first wives hadn't been subjected to this particular humiliation, why was I?

"I think you're wonderful, and I know you love my son. But I have to protect my business," Bernie replied.

I was an absolute bitch for those two days. I bombarded Mark with angry phone calls and messages, ruining his trip. I called Bernie. I consulted an attorney and had him call both Mark and Bernie. Finally, I was spent. Bernie won, and I had to be satisfied that I had made my point. I signed the agreement, and hoped Bernie and I could move past the ugliness.

As Mark and I celebrated our marriage that night in Nantucket, the wild autumn wind whipping outside, the videotape shows me spotting Bernie sitting off to the side alone, just watching. I march up to him and pull him onto the dance floor to the throbbing chorus of an old Eurythmics hit:

Sweet dreams are made of this.

Giddy and laughing, I dance with abandon, while Bernie shifts uncertainly from foot to foot, bewildered, looking for a way out.

· *three* ·

BECOMING A MADOFF

I thought the Madoffs were the perfect family. Everyone was smart, everyone seemed happy, everyone seemed to get along well enough. Madoffs moved through the world at cruising speed, never needing to shift gears or second-guess their direction, confident that the surface beneath them would remain solid and smooth. Disorder was the one thing that truly unhinged Bernie, and the life he had built reflected that—everyone and everything fell neatly into place. From the moment I became a Madoff, I struggled to find mine.

The whole concept of searching for yourself was alien to my husband. It was always a given that Bernie's sons would work for him someday, and presumably inherit Madoff Securities when he died. As soon as Mark graduated from the University of Michigan with his economics degree, he became his father's employee. When he and

Andy were given their own separate market-making division to run, they built a solid business that would earn them admiration on Wall Street as bright young stars in their own right. By their forties, Andy was restless, but Mark still loved working side by side with his brother after more than twenty years, and he enjoyed his work without becoming obsessive about it.

Mark couldn't have been any further from the ruthless Gordon Gekko stereotype of the successful young broker. When he walked through our apartment door around six each evening, he was done. He wasn't glued to his cell phone like his father, or answering client e-mails at the dinner table. Oddly enough, given his family name and the golden reputation it had then, Mark was never a person our friends would go to for stock tips. He was the one they'd go to for personal advice. It made sense, actually; he managed a hundred employees in a competitive, volatile business, and he did it with a velvet glove rather than an iron fist.

Keeping boundaries is part of being a successful manager, and Mark kept his work-related socializing to a minimum. He rarely entertained clients, and didn't go out for drinks with his work buddies at the end of the day, generally preferring to enjoy his single glass of Scotch each evening in the comfort of his own living room. We could have filled every night of the week with different charity events or see-and-be-seen social functions, but for the most part we were homebodies who preferred to stay in and watch *24* together on TV, go to bed early, and read. We were such huge *24* fans that Mark actually shed a couple of tears when the final episode aired. "Why are you crying?" I asked him, laughing.

"Because this show was just such a part of us," he replied ruefully.

Mark had once grabbed my black running shorts instead of his own while packing for a business trip, then decided to squeeze into them for a workout when he arrived, reasoning that no one else would be using the hotel gym at ten in the morning. He was mortified when he strutted in wearing his girl shorts only to find his TV hero, *24* star Kiefer Sutherland, staring back from a treadmill.

"Did you say anything to him?" I wanted to know.

"No," Mark admitted. "I was too embarrassed."

"You should've said you were wearing your wife's running shorts!" I teased.

Neither Mark nor I liked to dress up, and the only exception we were likely to make to our jeans-or-gym-clothes routine in the off-hours was for a mandatory charity dinner or auction to support cancer research. This had become a cause for the family since Andy's battle with lymphoma and the death from leukemia of Roger Madoff, the only son of Bernie's younger brother, Peter. Another young Madoff cousin was a cancer survivor, too. (I remember being at one of those silent auctions and Ruth wanted to buy me something. "Just pick something. Anything!" she urged. "C'mon, I need to find some way to enjoy this disease!")

Most evenings, Mark and I had dinner at some favorite neighborhood haunt, occasionally trying a new place Mark had noticed in a restaurant review. Despite his considerable resources, he hated to spend money unnecessarily and didn't have lavish tastes. He got his hair cut at the local barber, often flew coach unless we were vacationing with his parents and hitching a ride on their private jet, and bought cool but inexpensive bohemian-chic jewelry for me.

He wasn't a cheapskate by any means, and didn't believe in setting a household allowance, but I always consulted him before making any purchase over a few hundred dollars. If it was something major, like an antique or a dress for a special occasion, he would never refuse, but would always urge me to carefully think about it first. I had no problem with that. I wasn't a big shopper, anyway.

Eating out and going to the theater—Mark's deepest passion— were our biggest extravagances. Mark would see anything and everything onstage, including fringe productions where I would be snorting back a giggling fit in the front row during some overwrought monologue while he elbowed me in the ribs, urging me to stop. When he was being courted for the board of the Public Theater, we attended a dinner for the new creative director. Everyone was in earnest conversation about Billy Crystal's new one-man show, *700 Sundays*. I had fallen asleep during the acclaimed performance. "Stephanie," Mark had whispered, "he can see you! You have to stay awake!"

"So, Stephanie," one of the board members politely asked me, "what's some theater that you like?"

"My favorite play is Billy Joel's *Movin' Out*," I answered honestly. One of the things I loved most about Mark was his utter lack of pretension. He never expected me to perform, and he never tried to be anything other than his true self. Authenticity was more important to him than adulation. "Mr. Fun," he called himself in joking reference to his straight-arrow reputation.

Mark was an early riser, usually out of bed by five thirty a.m., instantly and thoroughly awake. He relished that quiet dawn hour or so to himself, and his routine never varied. He would brew whatever coffee had intrigued him at Starbucks that week, and the delicious aroma would waft through the apartment while he settled in to read the papers and e-mail articles he thought might be interesting to friends or family members—not financial news, but theater reviews, human interest pieces, travel stories, and such. He was an avid reader, and if he read a book he thought a friend might enjoy, he would send them a copy.

Once he was done with the morning news, Mark would make the same revolting smoothie for breakfast every single morning: yogurt, orange juice, frozen berries or mangoes, and prunes. I dozed through the whir of the blender out of self-defense; I had politely tried a sip or two of the "shit shake" to please him while we were dating, but once we were married, there was no way my stomach was making that sacrifice again. I would get up while he was showering, and he would greet me with eager plans for the evening. "Let me have a sip of coffee before you start asking where we should go for dinner," I would invariably protest. He'd kiss me good-bye and be out the door and on his way to the subway at seven thirty, the scent of his Old Spice lingering after he left. He wore that aftershave for as long as I knew him. I think he must have been seduced by the nautical theme. I loved the way he smelled.

Mark and I would chat by e-mail throughout the day; he was always sending me quick love notes or quotes ("Love is what makes two people sit in the middle of a bench when there's plenty of room at both ends"). He would usually try to slip away from his desk for a quick workout during the day; I was an exercise buff, too, but he was more focused on overall health than I was, and our different approaches were always laughably visible when it came to food. I would run ten miles on the treadmill and devour a big steak at dinner; Mark would have fish. Waiters were constantly mixing up our orders, assuming he was the one with the longshoreman's appetite.

Mark himself was a great chef, but cooking was something we liked to do on weekends, as an activity we could share. He was intuitive in the kitchen; I was a die-hard follower of recipes, once diligently following the "Chili for a Crowd" recipe in my *Silver Palate Cookbook* because it sounded so good, never mind the fact that I had a lobster pot full of chili for fifty people at the end of the day. "Why not cut the recipe?" Mark had suggested. I adamantly refused to change course, and true to his keep-the-peace nature, Mark backed down even though he knew he was right. We filled Tupperware containers with the leftovers, and he took them to work for his staff the next day. Food always disappeared fast on the trading floor. Twice a year, the company would host White Castle eat-offs, ordering five hundred burgers for the staff and then holding a contest to see who could eat the most in the least amount of time. Mark loved it purely as a spectator sport; he was too health-conscious to join in. His uncle Peter usually won.

There was a consistency and predictability to Mark that I found both reassuring and endearing. I'd dated my fair share of scumbags, cheats, and overgrown adolescents interspersed with some keepers, and I knew immediately that Mark was different from them all. From the very beginning, I didn't have to worry about any game-playing or secret agendas with Mark; he was honest and straightforward, to a fault at times. I knew he would never do anything to hurt me. There was a clarity to him, cool and clean as water. Mark Madoff would never be the life of the party, but you would enjoy having him there.

I think my occasional unpredictability appealed to him as much as his predictability did to me. My sense of humor and adventure was wackier and more impulsive than his, and I loved him all the more for not trying to mold me into some rich socialite wifey-wife. We always celebrated the anniversary of our first blind date, returning to the same restaurant where we had met that night. When I started talking about getting a tattoo around the anniversary of our Casimir date in 2007, Mark called me all excited. "You're not going to believe this, but the coolest tattoo parlor just opened next to Casimir," he reported. "Why don't we get your tattoo there after dinner?" We marched into the tattoo parlor as soon as we'd finished our meal that night.

"We're about to close," the tattoo guy said.

"I just want the outline of a star," I explained, pointing to my forearm.

"Okay," he agreed, "I guess I could do it, but I'm tired and I was out drinking all last night . . ."

We passed. The next morning, Mark woke up and the first thing he said was, "How bummed are you? You could've woken up with a tattoo!"

"I know!" I pouted.

I was still psyched to do it; I wanted to wear proof that I had that kind of courage, to flaunt it. After Mark left for work, I called the tattoo parlor and booked an appointment. When I arrived that afternoon, the proprietor appeared. His name was Alex. Every visible inch of his skin—and presumably what wasn't visible—was covered with tattoos, and his lobes had those big peg-hole piercings in them that make them droop like basset hound ears. He was bald, but not in a friendly-neighborhood-deli-guy bald way. He looked scary and mean and I sat there shaking all over. Another patron turned to me. He was about to endure a four-hour session to decorate the entire side of his torso, from armpit to hip.

"First time?" he asked.

"Yeah."

"What're you getting done?"

"Just an outline of a star."

"Oh, that'll take less than five minutes. Nothing to it. You bring an iPod?"

"No."

"You bring something to chew on while they're needling you?"

"Um, no."

He opened his meaty fist and slapped a piece of grape Hubba Bubba gum in my hand.

When it was over, I called Mark, exhilarated.

"I did it, I did it!"

"You're kidding," he said. He was surprised later to see that I'd opted to fill the star in instead of keeping it an outline ("The edges will round and blur," the tattoo artist had warned me), but he still loved it. I was cool, and he was vicariously cool. I debuted my ink at his daughter's bat mitzvah, and we both relished the *Oh my gaaaaawd* looks of horror on the faces of all the proper Connecticut wives there.

Despite my sense of derring-do, Mark was the one who was so secure about who he was, so confident that he was doing what he was meant to do, fulfilling a destiny that was clearly his. I envied that so much. Becoming a Madoff made me rethink not just who I was, but who I wanted to be. Maybe it was because I no longer had to search for love that I was driven to search for purpose. I had wanted to become a doctor since third grade, when I went on my first deep-sea fishing trip with my folks and watched my stepfather fillet our catch on board, pointing out the fish's organs to me as he worked. Biology fascinated me—science was my favorite subject throughout my school years. As an undergrad at Franklin & Marshall College, though, I majored in art and focused more on my social life than academics.

My parents pressured me to find a job as soon as I graduated, and life seemed to flow forth with no particular direction or design on my part after that. One of my stepdad's clients was John F. Kennedy Jr., and two weeks after I got my diploma, Marty was able to finagle an internship for me at *George*, the political lifestyle magazine John had just launched. It was all very hip and glamorous, and I managed to parlay the internship into a staff position, working my way through the junior ranks to associate photo editor. It was a young, tight-knit office that crackled with creative energy and high spirits—pranks were big, and the guys thought it was hilarious to lock me in the snack closet, which I would loudly protest but secretly look forward to.

More than anything, though, my three-year stint at *George* showed me there was a difference between following ambition and pursuing a passion. I was surrounded by brilliant people who believed fervently in what they were doing and were driven by a sense of purpose. We worked hard and played hard together, and for the first time, I felt like I was part of something exciting.

Despite his fame and the constant media attention, John was remarkably down-to-earth and approachable, the kind of boss who would bring back T-shirts or other little souvenirs for everyone on the staff whenever he returned from his latest trip to Vietnam or some other exotic place. The last time we saw him was at a routine staff meeting before he flew to Martha's Vineyard for his cousin Rory's wedding. When the small plane he was piloting disappeared that Friday night, we all clung to the hope that he had made it all up, that it was just some grand prank so he and Carolyn could escape the relentless paparazzi. We were heartbroken when searchers found the wreckage and then the bodies. *George* was quickly sold and went dark within a year. I bounced around a few women's magazines before a friend recommended me for the job with Narciso Rodriguez. It was fun, but not fulfilling once I was engaged and had the rest of my adult life to think about. I quit just before my wedding.

When we returned from our honeymoon in the Seychelles, I started casting about for something to do. I still desperately wanted to find my life's calling. I wanted to be able to say, "I'm a . . . ," but I didn't know how to fill in that blank. I just knew that "I'm a wife" was never meant to be my final, complete answer.

I remembered how much I had enjoyed a cake-decorating class I signed up for as a distraction years earlier after a boyfriend and I had broken up. Maybe I was the next Mrs. Fields and just needed to let my sweet tooth choose my life's path. I dropped in at the Institute of Culinary Education to look at their degree programs. "I think I might like to become a pastry chef," I told Mark that evening. I suspect, in hindsight, that it was really the idea of being in school—any school— that excited me. Now that I'm past the partying age, I could happily spend my life in college, pursuing degree after degree with no plans to graduate. Even buying school supplies gives me a rush. I wouldn't have balked as much as I did about registering for wedding gifts if Staples and a lifetime supply of colored index cards had been an option.

"If it's something you really want to do, Steph, you should do it," Mark said. "I just want you to do anything that makes you happy." He wouldn't even enjoy the fruits of my labor—he followed a gluten-free diet as a result of celiac disease, and his favorite dessert was sorbet. When he was courting me, he had totally charmed me by inviting me back to his place for dessert, which turned out to be a sorbet picnic on a blanket he spread in his living room, where he grandly arranged his little Häagen-Dazs tubs of orchard peach, mango, lemon, and strawberry.

For better or for worse, once I get an idea in my head, I immediately want to take action. Before I knew it, I was wearing a white chef's coat and learning everything you could possibly want to know about the molecular structure of a French baguette. My art degree came in handy when it came to decorating—I have proud memories and photographic evidence of perfect pink sugar roses and a whimsical white chocolate jellyfish with pulled-sugar tentacles—but my attention to detail didn't extend to the more mundane tasks. Making batter in gigantic industrial mixers sort of scared me, and a lot of the fun goes out of baking a cake when you're slamming out seventy of them in a single day.

This blind spot in my commitment became clear one afternoon when we were paired in teams to bake cakes and I was in charge of mixing the ingredients. When I pulled our cake out of the oven, my teammate looked stricken. Our classmates gathered around to inspect it. "That's a weird color," people kept saying (and not, I might add, in a supportive way—culinary students, I had discovered, are strangely intense). I studied my cake. They were right. Something didn't look right. We sliced it into samples for tasting, and everyone began spitting it out. As soon as I bit into my piece, I realized what I'd done: The recipe called for five cups of salt and ten cups of sugar; I'd reversed them.

I finished the five-month program, but bailed on the internship that was required to get a degree. Stick a fork in me, I was done.

Fortunately, I was able to put my identity crisis on hold temporarily, because finding a new place to live became a priority. Our apartment building had become one nightmare after another—management couldn't seem to conquer the rat problem or fix the temperamental elevator, and the apartment above ours was like a nightclub with the loud parties that kept us awake every weekend, which was odd, since it was supposedly owned by Swiss bankers. When our realtor showed us a loft around the corner on Mercer Street, we both gave a thumbs-up to the location and the space, but we hated the layout—the previous owners had put up too many walls, carving the airy great room into choppier, smaller spaces. The place had great bones, though, so we took it, and I threw myself into supervising renovations. We were halfway into the project when a slight redesign became necessary.

We were going to need a nursery.

I had known going into the relationship with Mark that there was a good possibility a divorced dad wouldn't want to have more children, and the more I fell in love with him, the more I convinced myself that I was okay with that, because we were so happy together. He was enough. And while I'd grown up assuming I'd have kids someday, I hadn't felt the physical baby-lust some of my friends had. The closest I'd come was when my puppy-clock went off and we ended up getting Grouper, right after the wedding.

In a weird way, it was Bernie and Ruth who unknowingly changed my mind about motherhood. Seeing the way they adored Kate and Daniel, as well as Andy's two daughters, I realized that I would never feel like we were a real family—or like I was a full-fledged member of theirs—without children of our own.

When I broached the subject, though, Mark was ambivalent. His visits with Kate and Daniel were every other weekend by then, plus Tuesday nights, and he liked the freedom that gave us. Did we really want to be tied down by a baby? And he was already forty—would it be fair for our child to have an "old" father? Mark was a worrier by nature, and he wondered whether he would be tempting fate, too. "I already have two healthy children," he would say, leaving the "what if" hanging out there darkly.

I couldn't disagree. We could move when and where we wanted, eat at great restaurants every day, and enjoy romantic weekends or vacations away. I had the perfect husband and the perfect life; I would have envied anyone who had what I had. But more and more of my friends were having kids, as well as the office wives I came to know casually through Mark's work, and my feelings on the subject were getting stronger and stronger. I wanted to be a mom.

I gently chipped away at Mark's reservations. He was outdoorsy, fit, and health-conscious; I'd seen him racing up and down the beach playing with the dog, and I had no fears whatsoever that he would be anything but an active, vibrant daddy. It was clear from his devotion to Kate and Daniel that Mark's greatest sense of self came from being a father, and his patient temperament made him a natural. He was so consistent and reliable that he had set his alarm for four every morning of our honeymoon so he could call his children and find out how their days at school had been. If we had a child of our own, I promised him, we would still be us, still have our life—I didn't want to be a shut-in mother tied to a Diaper Genie and Sesame Street videos— but our life would have a deeper purpose and meaning. I didn't just want to experience motherhood; I wanted to experience parenthood with him. Last but not least, I longed to give my own parents the kind of joy I saw in my in-laws when they were Papa Bernie and Granny Ruth.

When I told my ob-gyn I was interested in getting pregnant, he told me it takes the average couple a year, and that there were certain times of the month when I would be most fertile, blah blah blah. The only part of the lecture I paid attention to was the advice to "go have lots of sex." Mark and I headed off to Nantucket for a lovely off-season weekend. Back home, when my period failed to arrive exactly on schedule, I waited all of a single day before racing out to the drugstore. I was sure I felt this funny *zing* in my lower abdomen.

I bought every brand of pregnancy test on the shelf. I peed on e.p.t and got the two pink "yes" lines. Each box comes with two tests, so I repeated. "Yes" again! I tore open the Clearblue Easy box, this one was digital, and YES popped up on the tiny screen. Then I took both tests inside the First Response package—double YES again!

I had made dinner plans with a girlfriend that night, and we were due to meet in thirty minutes. I felt bad canceling at the last minute, so I left Mark a funny note and lined up all of the pregnancy tests next to it on the table, along with a bottle of tequila and a shot glass.

I figured he'd need a drink after seeing these results. On my way home from dinner, I popped into a bookstore and bought *What to Expect When You're Expecting* and a baby-name book. I'd never been happier or more excited in my life. I prayed Mark was feeling the same way. When I walked through the door, he greeted me with a bear hug, a huge grin on his face. "I'm really excited," he kept saying.

I loved being pregnant, though the thought of childbirth itself terrified me so much that my doctor actually advised me not to take any classes for fear it would stress me out too much. I signed up instead for BabyCenter's daily online newsletter, which told you what was going on with your body and offered helpful tips. I must have instantly deleted the ones focusing on prenatal nutrition. I basically craved anything that didn't fight back or run away first. I was hungry all day long.

For breakfast, I'd have an egg sandwich on a roll, a bagel with cream cheese, two or three bowls of Froot Loops or Apple Jacks, and a yogurt. I'd wash it down with a liter of pink grapefruit juice cocktail. Then I'd start thinking about lunch. Dirty dogs—hot dogs from one of New York's street vendors—were my favorite, and luckily, there was a cart just around the block. Heaping plates of pasta hit the spot, too. All of this was being piled onto an athletic five-feet-five frame I had proudly kept trim with daily workouts for my entire adult life. Four months into my pregnancy, I had gained thirty pounds. My doctor shook his head. "You know, Stephanie, you fucked yourself. You still have five months to go." I didn't care.

Our daughter was due December 4. When my brother got married that August, I looked like a giant watermelon with a blond bob, waddling down the aisle in my green bridesmaid dress. By the time I reached eight months, I weighed 186 pounds—more than Mark—and Bernie was making nasty remarks about the size of my rear end. Insensitive at best, but downright creepy when you stop to consider that your seventyish father-in-law has been eyeing your tuchus. Not that he could miss it at that point.

With a baby on the way, my nesting instincts kicked in big-time. I didn't just want the apartment done anymore, I wanted every detail to feel homey and "us," from the mounted wooden fish hung in our home office to the kitchen display of rolling pins I collected on eBay. We chose a deep, butter-soft leather sofa and matching chairs for the living room, and a rustic dining table that would accommodate the big holiday dinners I envisioned hosting for our extended family. Bernie and Ruth never entertained in their 64th Street penthouse—I was only over there twice in the eight years Mark and I were together—but they seemed to appreciate the family get-togethers we threw.

Bernie and Debbie didn't have a great relationship; Bernie complained bitterly to me that Andy's wife often ignored their visits, and sometimes would shut herself in another room when they came over to see the grandkids. I sympathized with him; I hadn't found Andy and Debbie to be particularly friendly or hospitable, either. Debbie was close friends with Susan and had met Andy through her. At one of Bernie and Ruth's parties in Montauk, she had parked herself in a lounge chair next to me while I was reading on the veranda and bluntly told me that we would never be friends because we just didn't have anything in common. I knew there were ongoing tensions in her marriage, which had to have been made even more stressful by Andy's battle with a rare form of lymphoma. And Debbie may well have been taking cover from Ruth to avoid her mother-in-law's occasional barbs. Ruth could take you down like a sniper. It wasn't necessarily malicious; she just never had a thought she didn't instantly express, and while the result was hilarious 99 percent of the time, that remaining 1 percent could leave you reeling. I remember when she gave me a lovely platinum chain for Hanukkah. As I opened the necklace, Ruth blithely explained that she had really wanted to get me a gorgeous evil-eye bracelet made of diamonds, blue topaz, and sapphires, "but I just couldn't bring myself to spend that kind of money on you."

Gift-giving was often an awkward affair in the extended Madoff family. They were generous people, but graciousness sometimes eluded them. I never once saw Bernie give his wife a gift; as far as I could tell, he didn't even get her birthday presents. "If I want something, I go out and buy it," Ruth matter-of-factly told me not long after we met. Neither mentioned that their wedding anniversary was on November 25, even though it undoubtedly fell on Thanksgiving sometimes.

It wasn't a mind-set I was used to. My family always made a big deal out of holidays and birthdays—I was the type who loved to keep an eye out for perfect little stocking stuffers all year round, and I like to give people presents that are meaningful, no matter how big or small. One of my first gifts to Mark was a tackle box full of handpicked flies. Part of showing how fond I am of someone is showing what I've come to know and love about them—their preferred pastimes, their favorite indulgences.

I'm also sentimental. I was touched when my mom thoughtfully included Kate in her tradition of giving a tiny Limoges box to each girl in the family for Christmas. Mom teases me about the dowry I brought to my marriage: my set of Twelve Days of Christmas plates and the silver punch bowl my grandfather had won in a golf tournament. Dumb, but they mattered to me.

Bernie and Ruth were impulsive shoppers. Once, while visiting them in Palm Beach, we were strolling downtown when I decided to duck into a store to look at some sandals and sundresses for an upcoming Mexican vacation Mark and I had planned. Bernie walked up to the counter and slapped down his credit card.

"Anything she touches, she gets," he announced grandly to the beaming salesclerk, as if I were some Mafia princess. I was mortified.

"Bernie, no, really, thank you, that's ridiculous, I can buy my own clothes," I protested. He insisted, then left his credit card there and wandered off. Ruth and I picked out a few things, and Bernie reappeared.

"Where were you?" Ruth demanded.

"I went across the street to Hermès," he said.

"Bernie, *that's* where you should have told Stephanie she could buy anything," Ruth shot back. As usual, Bernie let his wife's sarcasm roll off his back.

While the Madoffs themselves may have sent confusing, sometimes bumbling messages with their gift-giving habits, it was obvious from both our wedding and Audrey's baby shower that largesse was something that was expected from Bernie's clients. One Madoff client bought my entire set of wedding china. Another sent a silver Napoleon-era baby rattle from France for Audrey. Before both events, the doorman sent up more and more boxes daily from Tiffany, Cartier, Barneys, Hermès, and other luxury stores, invariably from people we'd never met and probably never would. It was mind-boggling.

Yet when I went to BuyBuy Baby with two girlfriends before Audrey was born, to stock up on all the baby basics in one fell swoop, Bernie took one look at all the bags in our vestibule and made some derogatory comment about my spending being out of control. It hit a nerve, because I was hardly a spendthrift. I wasn't about to waltz into Prada and drop thousands on a few cashmere sweaters the way I'd seen him do. We weren't talking Frette crib sheets or Belgian Lace christening gowns here; it was bottles, sterilizers, and burp cloths from a discount chain. Maybe my hormones were making me hypersensitive, but it didn't seem Bernie's place to begrudge me a breast pump.

Mark's children were excited about a new little sister on the way, and I hoped the baby would bring us closer together. Maybe if we were more clearly defined as a nuclear family, Mark's ex would back off and stop acting as if our life was hers to arrange whenever we had Kate and Daniel. Her imperious style was hard to take. I remember that when iPods first came out, I had been all excited about getting one for Kate and Daniel as our big Hanukkah gift that year. Susan caught wind of it somehow, and when she dropped the kids off at our Greenwich house one weekend before the holidays, she pointed at Mark and me and barked a command: "You and you, in the kitchen. Now!" She slammed the door behind her before ripping into us. She did not want the kids to have iPods and we had no business getting them. She had consulted a child psychologist who knew the family, and the psychologist also opposed it. I stood there dumbfounded; Mark began chewing his nails. Once she left, I turned on him.

"How could you let this woman scream at me in my own home?" I demanded, not stopping to ask myself the same question. Mark's answer was the same as it always was: She was their mother, and if he pushed back, the relationship with his children might suffer. But he must have smoothed things over later, because we did end up buying the iPods. Before we could give them to Kate and Daniel, however, Susan made sure they got their Hanukkah gifts from her: all the iPod accessories. If she was going to lose the battle, she was at least going to make sure our victory was short-lived and ruin the surprise.

When it came time for Daniel's bar mitzvah, the behind-the-scenes drama was bad enough to send Mark and me into couples therapy in search of a healthy way to handle relations with his ex. We had to stop walking on eggshells all the time. Mark was averse to disciplining the kids, not even putting his foot down over homework when they were with us. If we were having a quiet conversation in the corner of the family room while they were watching one of their shows, we got shushed and stayed shushed. When I made some light comment once about the kids being spoiled (something I was guilty of doing to them, too), Mark totally lost it. "How dare you speak that way about my children!" he railed. I became adept at quietly storing my criticisms and resentments, until the pressure built and I exploded. It was an exhausting, destructive pattern.

My breaking point came over the rehearsal dinner Susan insisted on having the night before the bar mitzvah. She wanted everyone there: her parents and brothers, Mark and me, Andy and his family, my brother, my parents, and Bernie and Ruth. To their credit, Bernie and Ruth could pleasantly fake their way through any forced encounter with former or estranged daughters-in-law for the sake of their beloved grandkids. Susan never saw Bernie grimacing when she threw her arms around him in a hug, and Debbie never heard his complaints about how rude or cold she was. I wanted nothing to do with these grand charades, though. I felt uncomfortable around Susan and her family, and I didn't particularly want to subject my parents and brother to such an awkward situation, either. Why couldn't we all just be together at the bar mitzvah? If Susan wanted a rehearsal dinner with her family, she was welcome to just do it on her own, obviously. "It's ridiculous," I complained to Mark. "Why doesn't anyone accept that you're divorced?"

Counseling proved to be no help. I would blow up, and Mark would blow up. But I could feel better after venting, walk out, and move on with the day. Mark held on to his hurt and anger for a week at a time. He just could not let go. It was taking too great a toll on him; it wasn't worth it. We agreed on a compromise: I would suck it up this time in exchange for Mark's firm promise that there would be no faux-family reunion rehearsal dinner reprise at Kate's bat mitzvah a couple of years down the road.

I was going to be a parent myself soon enough, but when I went for my weekly checkup on November 20 and asked if I was close to delivery, my obstetrician didn't mince words. "Stephanie, this baby is closer to your nose than your vagina." I left the appointment and met my mom for lunch, then lumbered over to Whole Foods. I was hosting Thanksgiving in a couple of days, and I needed ingredients for my stuffing. The store was jammed. I picked up a few things and headed home, looking forward to the prenatal massage Mark had booked for me that evening. Afterward, I was ready for bed.

"I don't feel well. My tummy really hurts," I remarked.

By eleven thirty, the pain was coming and going. I woke Mark and got our copy of *What to Expect When You're Expecting*.

"Stephanie, if you were in labor, you couldn't even walk, trust me," Mark said through a yawn. I figured he knew more about it than I did and let him go back to sleep. The dull pain kept coming and going, coming and going, and finally I got up to go lie on the couch to see if I could get comfortable there. Grouper roused himself from his dog bed and trailed after me. I mentally replayed my last conversation with the obstetrician.

"If I go into labor, what do I do?" I had asked.

"Whatever you do, Stephanie," he had replied, "don't call me in the middle of the night." We both knew I was paranoid enough about going into labor that I was bound to overreact to the slightest false alarm. But after reviewing the labor symptom checklist in the book that night, and Googling "going into labor" on the computer, I was pretty sure this was no false alarm. But it wasn't cinematic, Scarlett-

O'Hara-in-labor agony, either, so I let both my husband and my doctor enjoy their night's sleep.

When the waves of pain still hadn't subsided by three thirty in the morning, I thought, *I want to look good when my daughter is born. I'm going to take a shower and do my hair.* By now, Mark was awake, too.

"If you're in that much pain, I think we should call the doctor," he suggested. I decided to wait a bit longer. At five thirty, I finally caved and dialed the number. After describing what had been going on for the past six hours, the doctor had only one question: "Where are you?"

"Home," I replied, surprised he would wonder.

"Come to the hospital!"

I burst into tears. Crying and suddenly terrified, I called my parents as we grabbed a cab and shot up to Mount Sinai Hospital, arriving around six thirty. I was whisked into Labor and Delivery.

"Tell your parents to go home, it's going to be a long day," the doctor said after discovering I was only four centimeters dilated. My mom decided to listen to her own instincts and refused to budge. When it came time to push, Mark spent the entire forty-five minutes holding my hand, with his lips pressed to my forehead. His other hand was supporting my leg, which was hoisted somewhere north of my ears. I wasn't entirely sure, because I couldn't feel it, thanks to the epidural.

"Here she comes, here she comes!" the doctor cried. Mark went white as a sheet, dropped my leg with a thud, and bolted behind the pink maternity-ward curtain, certain he was about to faint. Audrey was born at 11:19 a.m. Mark poked his head back around the curtain, quickly declining to cut the cord. I thought it was too cute that a guy who could fillet a just-caught hundred-pound tuna on the deck of a boat was squeamish about an umbilical cord.

"Can I do it?" I asked.

"Forget it," the doctor replied.

The baby was put in a warmer and came back swaddled and beautiful. Mark greeted his daughter properly, with a huge, proud smile.

My own happiness was indescribable in that moment. As they wheeled my gurney down the hall on the way to my room, I shouted out for anyone and everyone to hear: "I just had a baby, and I wanna do it again!"

Bernie and Ruth were in France, but jumped on a private jet as soon as they heard the news, and were in the hospital by eight that night to meet their new granddaughter. Audrey Viola Madoff was seven pounds, ten ounces, with spiky black hair and her father's eyes. We brought her home, fittingly enough, on Thanksgiving Day. Mark was an amazing father, so in love he would race to change a dirty diaper or pick her up at the first hint of a whimper. His hands were always on her. He wrote me tender love notes, thanking me for the wonderful gift that was our daughter.

The grandparents were all predictably smitten, too. I remember one lunchtime when Bernie called, asking if he could come over to give Audrey a bottle. He was downtown on business and had his driver bring him by. He sat on the sofa in his custom French-tailored Charvet shirt and exquisite tailored suit, cradling the baby in his arms as Audrey guzzled her milk. It's one of the more difficult memories I have of him, because it's impossible to reconcile the tenderness with the cruelty, to acknowledge what he gave without remembering what he took. And what he took from my children can never be forgiven.

Audrey was nineteen months old when the little pink lines on another pregnancy test confirmed that a sibling was on the way. It was the summer of 2008, and Mark and I had been enjoying warm, lazy weekends whenever we could at the gray-shingled house we'd bought on the water at Tom Nevers Beach in Nantucket. It was a place I envisioned being in our lives forever. Our daughter would get married there someday, and Mark and I would become the sweet old couple locals would see out fishing every day. I dreamt of having friends and family members streaming through all summer long, having barbecues on the beach and big Sunday breakfasts. News of another baby on the way had brought shouts of joy from my parents, and I couldn't wait to tell Bernie and Ruth, too. I decided that Audrey would be the perfect messenger.

We waited until the annual Madoff Montauk party. When we arrived at the house the day before for a family dinner, Audrey and I found Ruth puttering in the kitchen and Bernie getting ready to barbecue. I had put my art skills to work and made a card for Audrey to give them, announcing that she was going to be a big sister. When it was time for the big moment, Ruth took the card from Audrey's tiny hands, opened it, read it, and hollered to her husband in her thick Queens accent: "Hey, Berrrrrnie. Stephanie's pregnant. Bet you never saw that coming, huh?" Audrey stood there confused, then toddled away. Ruth and Bernie hugged us, but there were no tears of joy this time or champagne corks flying.

My mother had mentioned that Ruth didn't seem her vivacious self that summer. My parents had a home not far from the Madoffs' beach house in Montauk, and the two couples had gotten together for lunch or dinner five or six times at the Chowder House, a local favorite. Ruth had confided to my mom she was very concerned about Bernie. He didn't seem well. I thought something was strained about both of them that day we announced my second pregnancy. The deadened reaction was completely out of character for two people who loved being grandparents as much as they did. Something was definitely off-kilter.

My own bearings, though, were strong as could be. I finally had the perfect word to fill in that nagging personal blank: *I am,* I told myself, *a mother.* Nothing could possibly have felt more right.

My children had opened my eyes to a career path that also felt right. My lost dream of medical school had prompted me to apply to be a volunteer in a renowned hospital's pediatric oncology ward. The vetting process had taken six months, with interviews, background checks, blood tests, and two orientations before I was approved to help in the Child Life department. Child Life Specialists are part of a hospital's psychosocial care team, working closely with patients and families to cope with the serious illness of a child. They help their young patients adjust to the hospital environment and prepare them for the tests and procedures they will face, using techniques such as play and art therapy. My job was basically to provide support in the outpatient playroom, overseeing the arts and crafts table and helping the kids with individual or bigger group projects. I would also go sit by a child's bedside if a parent needed to duck out for a few minutes, or to offer whatever companionship might make a sick child feel better. A little girl in pain after surgery once asked me to just rub her feet for her, so I sat at the end of her bed and massaged them until she was soothed.

Privacy laws prevented me from knowing the details of what every small patient was going through, but I could see the fear and fatigue in the parents' faces. The child life experts warn volunteers from the beginning that the burnout rate is high, because the work is so emotionally draining. But I had the opposite reaction. Contrary to warnings, I found the atmosphere on the pediatric floor charged with hope and optimism. It wasn't about dying, it was about fiercely being alive. Here were families caught in the worst crisis imaginable, yet they were still laughing, still living, still holding on to one another with a strength that was almost defiant.

Life, they showed me, could go on no matter how unpredictable, no matter how unfair.

· *four* ·

OPTICAL ILLUSIONS

Mark never saw his father in person again after storming out of his parents' apartment the day Bernie confessed to his monstrous lies. The day after blowing the whistle on Bernie's Ponzi scheme, Mark and Andy spent hours meeting with Martin Flumenbaum, a top New York trial lawyer who had been a longtime friend and former partner of Marty's. Together they met with SEC officials and investigators from the U.S. Attorney's Office, answering whatever questions they could about Bernie and his business.

I spent the bleak day at home, going through the motions of my normal routine by rote, watching a cold rain fall from a gray sky and waiting to see what would happen next. Feeling the flutter-kicks that morning of the baby due in seven weeks, I began to wonder what kind of life we would be able to salvage for him and his two-year-old sister. Would we be stripped of everything we owned? Would my husband be called to testify against his own father at trial? Had Ruth known anything at all?

The amount of money Bernie had meticulously and mercilessly stolen over the course of a decade or more was nothing short of staggering—a reported $65 billion taken from thousands of trusting friends, relatives, investors, organizations, and charitable foundations. Beyond the fortune lost, though, no investigator, auditor, or attorney would ever be able to tally the true damage Bernie did, the hurt and despair he caused his victims, the lives he destroyed. He swindled my own parents out of a part of their retirement savings, and heartlessly did the same to members of his own family. Hundreds of innocent employees who had nothing to do with the elite and imaginary private fund Bernie managed nonetheless lost their livelihoods and their professional reputations, their résumés rendered toxic because they had worked for the biggest con man in history.

On December 11, the day of his father's arrest, Mark returned home before the five-o'clock news looking spent.

"Where do you think your dad is?" I had to ask. "Is he in jail yet?"

We would later learn that two FBI agents had appeared at Bernie's door around seven thirty that Thursday morning. Bernie was about to get dressed for work. I imagined him standing there in his vast walk-in closet, surrounded by the shirts he had tailor-made in Paris, by the tidy rows of Hermès suits and Prada coats and hundreds of fussy Belgian loafers, everything compulsively arranged by color, not a hanger out of place. Bernie's outward disdain for any hint of mess-iness also carried over to his office, where he insisted that every desk be kept pristine; to his yacht, where only clean, bare feet were allowed to touch the gleaming floors; to the impeccably formal penthouse, where visitors, including his own children and grandchildren, were rarely welcomed, lest they track in dirt or spill a drink. Padding up-stairs in his robe and slippers to greet the agents, Bernie had calmly confirmed what Mark and Andy had told authorities. "There is no innocent explanation," he reportedly said before changing into a well-cut suit and being taken into custody. Even his downfall was precise and orderly. The rest of us were left to be consumed by the chaos he unleashed.

Our lives stopped belonging to us from the moment Mark turned his father in. Suddenly we weren't Mark and Steph anymore. We weren't individuals, or a couple, or a young family. We were a crisis to manage. From that day forward, virtually every decision would be made for us, every action or inaction dictated to us by our lawyers or the media consultants they insisted we hire. We would become mired in litigation for crimes we did not commit. Overnight, a new word would come to dominate our everyday existence: *optically*.

Optically, we were told, we should not be seen shopping. Opti-cally, it wasn't a good idea to eat out. Optically, going to the theater or a concert was out of the question. How we might be perceived took precedence over who we actually were. We weren't in any mood to go out, anyway, but the mandate added to the shame we already felt carrying the Madoff name. My good friend RoseMarie, a public relations consultant who had worked with me at *George* magazine, sounded the first warning: "Stephanie, I don't care if you have a bag from Kmart, I don't want you to be seen with it."

I saw what she meant within a few days, when the tabloids ran photos of Andy and his girlfriend (misidentified as his wife in the caption) shopping in SoHo, their arms full of bags from trendy stores. No matter that Andy and Mark had exposed their father's fraud and were not accused of any wrongdoing themselves, the implied message was clear: Madoffs still prosper while destitute victims suffer. In a matter of weeks, I began buying even basic household necessities like toothpaste online, to be delivered discreetly to our door, past the clutch of reporters and photographers now keeping vigil on the sidewalk outside.

The protective doormen in the lobby became our loyal lookout team, calling us with updates: "Three reporters on Mercer and a photographer sleeping in his car." Mark easily eluded the scrum by slipping out a back door that opened onto the street behind our building, leaving before seven each morning to meet with lawyers. At first, the media presence made me nervous, but I soon realized no one knew who I was unless I was with Mark, anyway. Our low-key social life and disinterest in being part of the rich young jet-setter scene turned out to have its own rewards. I could take Grouper out for his walks and even stop and smile as the bored reporters scratched his ears; they had no clue the pregnant woman with the huge dog and a pooper-scooper was their quarry's wife.

It would all die down once Bernie was locked up, our legal team promised; we just needed to keep our heads down and move forward. We were in the middle of a tornado, they said, but it would pass quickly. When Mark got home each day, he would scour the Internet for news and read personal e-mails, which he shared with me only if they were words of support and encouragement. I was getting bombarded myself with voice mails, texts, and e-mails from concerned friends and curious acquaintances, too, but both Mark and I were under strict orders to say nothing to them beyond the carefully scripted statement the lawyers had prepared: *Thank you for your concern. We are in shock and victims of Bernie's crimes as well.*

Mark never went back to the Lipstick Building. His staff was still working—it takes time to close down a brokerage firm—while investigators aggressively searched all three floors. A coworker phoned to say that she had packed up a couple of boxes of photos, knickknacks, and other personal belongings from Mark's office if he wanted to pick them up. "I can't go back there," Mark decided. His belongings were sent via messenger to his attorney's office instead.

Our apartment turned into a sort of bunker. Mark and I cooked or ordered in and spent idle hours debating whether "the old guys"— Bernie's four top lieutenants—had known all along about the Ponzi scheme. We kept waiting for more arrests to happen. We tried to figure out when Bernie's double life as a con man had likely begun, the riddle that bothered Mark most. Had the charade gone on for five years, ten years, his whole life? What had triggered it?

By the end of the first emotionally exhausting week after Bernie's arrest, Mark ached to see Kate and Daniel. The change of scenery would do us both good. We packed up Audrey and the dog and headed to Greenwich for a weekend escape from the bad-news epicenter. As soon as we got to Connecticut, though, Mark's phone began to ring. His eyes widened when he saw the number flash across the screen. His face tightened.

"Oh my God. It's my mother," he said. Neither of us had heard from Ruth since Mark and his brother had confronted Bernie. Remembering later how Ruth had sat through the ugly scene as blank-faced as a zombie, Mark had had the distinct impression that she wasn't hearing Bernie's confession for the first time. Our lawyers had advised us not to have any contact with either Bernie or Ruth as the investigation unfolded; her role in the whole affair was still unclear. Mark answered his mother's call anyway, not knowing what to expect.

She wanted to know if Mark would post bail for his father. The judge was demanding a $10 million bond.

There were no angry accusations, no bitter recriminations, no apologies. Ruth made the request as if she were asking a maître d' to validate a parking ticket. She was obviously in a state of deepest denial. Unwilling or unable to confront his mother, Mark mumbled something vague about talking to his attorneys and quickly ended the conversation. He hung up, dumbfounded and furious. What on earth was she thinking? Did she not realize what Bernie had done, how thoroughly he had betrayed his family, how cavalierly he had put us all in harm's way? Bernie was seventy years old. It was clear from the moment he surrendered that he would die behind bars. Ruth wasn't standing by her man. She was standing by a monster.

I hated Bernie thoroughly and deeply from the instant Mark told me what he had done. There was no gradual coming to terms with it, no feeling conflicted or torn. The emotion hit me instantly, a full-force missile. I'd had genuine affection for my father-in-law. Now I cringed to think how endearing I had found it that a supposedly self-made billionaire—reputedly one of the wealthiest men in the world—favored hamburgers over caviar and went to the movies every evening with a woman he had begun dating half a century ago. I had been proud that he was such a revered figure in the business world, and so delighted that I knew the "real" Bernie. Now, nothing about him was real. Every fond memory felt suspect. That whole wonderful, fairy-tale family life I had so eagerly embraced seemed like it had never been anything but one big masquerade ball, planned and choreographed by Bernie Madoff. He had played us all.

That my husband might somehow have been involved in Bernie's criminal operation never once crossed my mind. He and Andy ran a completely separate business, and I have vivid memories of the two or three times in all our years together that Mark ever came home late at the end of a working day. Each time, he recounted having had the same blowup with his father—a rare event to begin with, but in hindsight, these arguments were telling. The last one had been the summer before Bernie's arrest, when family members had had their first inklings that something wasn't right with Bernie and had been concerned about his health.

"I had a huge fight with my dad," Mark announced one evening a few months before Bernie's arrest.

"About what?"

Mark launched into a litany I had heard before. "Stephanie, my dad is getting older. He doesn't eat right, he doesn't exercise, he doesn't take care of himself, and he won't even go to the doctor for checkups. His own father dropped dead of a heart attack at fifty-five. I'm worried, because I don't have any clue what he does and how he does it, what his end of the business is. If he drops dead, I just want to know what I should do." Whenever he asked his father to explain his private fund and how the golden egg of Wall Street was managed, though, Bernie balked.

"You do your job and I'll do mine," he would snap. Mark didn't understand. Bernie seemed pleased by the separate business his sons had built. Why wouldn't he want them to learn more?

Andy was losing interest in the family business, anyway, and wanted to pursue other passions, like fund-raising for his favorite lymphoma research foundation or running the little fishing-reel business in which he and Mark had become partners. The prospect of Andy's leaving made Mark feel all the more responsible as heir apparent to their father's multibillion-dollar business. He felt insulted that Bernie was so dismissive, as if he didn't consider him smart enough or competent enough to fill his shoes.

"Let him cool down a bit, then see if you can approach it again," I'd suggested. I always found Bernie to be so sweet and soft-spoken. It was hard to imagine him confronting anyone and raising his voice, let alone saying anything demeaning to his son. I could see why Mark was hurt and baffled.

Bernie would always imply in later interviews and interrogations that he had been protecting his sons by erecting an impenetrable firewall between his legitimate business, which the boys ran, and his criminal operation, which he alone oversaw. But that explanation, like everything else Bernie has had to say, boils down to self-serving spin control.

When he confessed to Mark and Andy, Bernie told them he had hundreds of millions of dollars still at hand, which he intended to use for checks made payable to select family members, friends, and employees. He was planning to distribute that money before he turned himself in, but his sons unwittingly forced his hand when they challenged their father about his inexplicable decision to pay out the firm's annual bonuses that December instead of the usual February. Bernie had to have seen the same danger that Mark and Andy instantly did with his proposed game plan of waiting a week to turn himself in: It would have made his sons unwilling co-conspirators. Telling them about the Ponzi scheme and then expecting them to sit idly by while he proceeded to steal and disperse another couple of hundred million dollars only showed how cold and arrogant Bernie truly was. Aiding and abetting him would make his children criminals, too, and whether he truly intended to turn himself in or perhaps intended to suck funds for his criminal venture from Mark and Andy's legitimate one is anyone's guess. Investigators found approximately $140 million in signed "bonus" checks in a desk drawer when they raided Bernie's office. That was a $140 million holdup-in-progress that my husband and his brother stopped.

I felt enormously proud that I was with the man who did the right thing. Bernie was the unimpeachable financial genius, the sage patriarch who was admired by his peers and worshipped by his son. Mark put him on a pedestal and had always counted on Bernie for advice, approval, and unconditional love. To have an entire lifetime of trust destroyed in a single moment was devastating, and for Mark to have found the strength in that moment to set his own betrayal aside and fight back on behalf of all Bernie's victims took a kind of courage not everyone has. I never doubted Mark's innocence for a single second. He was a hero.

But Mark was too engulfed in his own pain to feel any of that pride himself. The press never bothered to put two and two together and draw the obvious conclusion about Mark. Sensationalism ruled the day. If your name was Madoff, you were a crook; it was as simple, and as unjust, as that. I watched my decent, gentle husband be consumed by the same soul-searing rage I felt for Bernie, along with a sorrow that was a hundred times worse.

The emotional blow physically changed Mark from the very first day. His athletic shoulders curled inward, hunching him like an old man, and his boyishly handsome face aged overnight, too. A fault line of anger and distrust crossed his forehead. He looked drawn and haggard. He grew a beard that came in gray and white, and he began wearing his glasses even when he didn't need them, just to disguise himself. The smile that made me fall in love with him disappeared altogether. "Was my life real?" he would often ask. We would never know. The one person who could answer that was the biggest liar in the world.

My parents and younger brother, Rob, were our greatest source of comfort in the aftermath of the catastrophe Bernie created. Mark had always had a great relationship with Pinks and Marty, and now my parents became his. He and Marty grew especially close, with Marty offering not only his love and support, but his wise counsel as well. They talked several times a day, and Marty responded instantly to every frantic e-mail Mark sent in between. Whenever some news development sent Mark into a tailspin, Marty would patiently interpret the legalese, separate fact from rumor, and urge Mark yet again to stay away from the computer.

Far worse than the breathless tabloid reports and supposed news stories riddled with errors were the comments attached to them online. Vicious, unsubstantiated rumors and outright lies became part of the cyberspace archive of Mark David Madoff. I could laugh off fabricated reports about our so-called lavish lifestyle as they appeared in the press and then move on with my day, but Mark couldn't. "Can't you just tell your side of the story?" I wondered naïvely.

"They won't let me!" he cried. The lawyers and crisis managers, he meant. Our highly paid puppeteers. Optically, they advised, it was best to keep our silence, no matter how frustrating. Making a comment would only inflame the mob. As my stepfather observed, "It's blood they want, not justice."

My mother wasn't as worried about optics as she was about me. I was trying hard to focus on my pregnancy; carrying Audrey had been such pure joy, and I was determined to re-create that experience with this baby. Bernie had ruined everything else in our lives—he wasn't getting my mother-to-be glow as well. Mark and I had been ecstatic when we found out the baby was a boy; I had been so keen to have a son that I had followed every old wives' tale and Internet suggestion out there, even making Mark drink Diet Coke before trying to conceive. (I had heard that it made sperm swim faster, and since male sperm were known to die sooner, I wanted them to have the competitive edge in this particular race.)

Our son was due March 1. A week after Bernie's arrest, my mother suggested we go uptown to Lester's, the store where she had taken me shopping for Audrey's layette. That had been such a fun, special mother-daughter day. My mom was eager now to coax me out of the house and provide a few hours of happy distraction from all the drama. "C'mon, it'll be fun," she cajoled. "I want to do this for you."

In the Lester's baby section, I picked out some onesies and receiving blankets, washcloths and tiny undershirts, trying to lose myself in the sweet moment, to summon the excitement I had felt the first time. It felt forced. My mother oohed and aahed over each item, trying to bring me around. She paid for everything, and I arranged to have it mailed to me. Optics.

On the way home, Mom and I decided to grab a bite to eat, and stopped at a nearby diner to have grilled cheeses and French fries. We settled into a booth by the window. There was the usual lunch-hour background noise—plates clattering, waitresses calling orders, customers chatting, blather from a TV mounted on the wall. Suddenly the incredulous voice of a woman sitting near us carried across the tables. "Sixty-five billion dollars, *shit!*" I looked up and saw Bernie's mug flash across the TV screen. He had the same lipless smirk as the Grinch Who Stole Christmas. My mom and I locked eyes and grimaced. At the same time, I caught a glimpse of Bernie's face filling the cover of the *New York Post* that another diner was holding open. THE MOST HATED MAN IN NEW YORK, the headline screamed. I felt the weight of Bernie settle back over me, over my small family. He had us pinned. We couldn't escape him no matter how hard we tried.

One evening, Mark and I had ordered in Chinese food and were watching television in the living room when we heard the jingling of the sleigh bells I had used to decorate the inside of our front door. Someone was in the house. We'd neglected to lock the door after our take-out was delivered. Mark bolted for the elevator, with me close behind. I rounded the corner into the foyer to hear him saying, "Yes?" and then politely adding, "I have no comment. You can contact my attorney, Martin Flumenbaum." A woman from the *New York Post* cowered in the elevator while Mark held back Grouper, who was going ballistic. I couldn't believe Mark was being gracious to a tabloid reporter who had just barged into our home. "What is wrong with you? What do you want?" I yelled at her while Mark held me back, a protective hand across my hugely pregnant belly.

Christmas that year was sad and subdued, with Mark and me putting on a show for Audrey's sake. She had just turned two, and the thrilling idea of someone named Santa showering her with presents was just starting to take hold. Our tree had been up and decorated a few days before Bernie's confession, and on Christmas Eve I filled the stockings dutifully, too numb to feel any of my usual delight. Mark and my stepdad had spent so many long days together going over the case that they had become cocktail-hour Scotch buddies, and I tucked miniature bottles in each of their stockings as a joke.

That year, I had stashed away a little game called The Elf on the Shelf months before the holidays. I was charmed by the story of an elf assigned to each child by Santa himself, sent to sit in secret places throughout the house in the days leading up to Christmas to see whether the child was behaving herself. Each day, the elf would be hidden in a different spot for the child to find. The idea of starting such a cute tradition for my daughter had tickled me, but now I couldn't even bring myself to take the elf out of his box. The anticipation I usually felt surrounding Christmastime had been replaced by a sense of growing dread. *Well, next Christmas will be better,* I consoled myself. Maybe the elf could make his debut then.

Hanukkah proved to be an even worse disaster. Instead of the usual party I always hosted for my Jewish in-laws and the kids in Connecticut, Mark and I decided to have an intimate, private celebration with Kate and Daniel. I was looking forward to the relative freedom Greenwich would give us. Mark's paranoia about the press was so bad that he wanted to keep all the blinds in the loft drawn in case there were photographers on the roof of the building across the street. I drew the line at spending my day in a big, dim cave. We packed the car up with all the gifts, plus the groceries I had bought for a special dinner, and set off, planning on a quick stop along the way to have my blood pressure checked at my obstetrician's office uptown. We weren't even halfway to the doctor's before Mark got a call. He hung up and turned to me, his face white as chalk.

"That was Andy. He's heard from a reliable source that death threats have been made against us."

I burst into tears. Was Audrey in danger, too? What if someone tried to hurt my little girl, or snatch her?

"I'm so scared. This is crazy," I cried. "I'm so scared, Mark. What are we supposed to do?"

Mark looked equally terrified. We pulled up to the doctor's office. "Go to your appointment," he urged me. "I'm going to give Marty Flumenbaum a call."

I wiped my eyes and went inside, too scared and embarrassed to confide in my doctor when he looked at my numbers. "It's slightly elevated," he said. I felt a small sense of relief; if a death threat wasn't sending my blood pressure through the roof, it was probably safe to assume nothing would.

"Marty is calling the authorities," Mark reported when I got back into the car. We just sat there for a few minutes, trying to figure out what to do. "Fuck it," Mark finally said, peeling too fast out of the parking spot. "We're going back to the apartment. I'm too scared to stay at the house." The house in Greenwich was too isolated. We would be safer in SoHo, he reasoned. At least no one could break in through the windows there, and we had the added security of a doorman.

In the elevator on the way up to our apartment, Mark was still playing out horrible scenarios. "Of course, if someone comes and puts a gun to the doorman's head, they'd be able to get into the apartment," he pointed out.

"We have to get a bodyguard," I pleaded. "We need some security." I felt panicked. Andy had immediately applied for a license to buy a gun, and he hired muscle as well. Should we do the same? Authorities soon confirmed that there had indeed been "some chatter" out there about killing us, but Mark still hesitated to hire protection. He relayed the lawyers' reassurances: It's not at that point, yet.

Yet? I wondered. This was all supposed to die down in a few weeks. When had *yet* come into play? I kept pushing Mark, but he didn't want to spend the money. And there was public perception to keep in mind, too. Optically, a bodyguard wasn't a good idea. If I was really that worried, Mark suggested, he could arrange for one of the now jobless Madoff drivers we trusted—a formidably big man named Errol—to escort Audrey and me to her day care. I backed down. Mark and I were already stressed-out enough, and I didn't want this to become a fight between us. And on some subconscious level, I suppose, I thought that faking normalcy would somehow restore it, by sheer force of will.

I knew our nightmare was nothing compared to Ruth's. The drumbeat of accusations surrounding Mark and Andy—the sons must have known, the confession was staged, they're hiding something— rained down around Ruth as well, and her blind devotion to Bernie riled everyone up even more. Bernie had been released on his own recognizance and a $10 million bond that required four cosigners willing to pledge their assets on his behalf. Ruth and his brother, Peter, had signed, but Mark and Andy had both refused. Anyone Bernie might count as a close friend had been ripped off by him, and he didn't find anyone else to cosign; "the most hated man in New York" went back to court unable to meet the judge's conditions for his freedom.

A deal was worked out again, and Bernie was allowed to go back home with a curfew, and later an electronic ankle bracelet. The official restrictions were moot, anyway—the hordes of reporters and gawkers outside his building made it virtually impossible for him to leave, and even if he did slip out for a while, it wasn't as if he could stroll the streets of New York freely. He and Ruth were instantly recognized, and universally hated. I was relatively certain that Ruth had not been complicit in Bernie's white-collar robbery, and my heart broke for her. The media wanted a dragon lady, like one of those greedy shoe-and-diamond-hoarding wives of brutal dictators. Ruth had her shortcomings, but she wasn't in that league, and didn't deserve the beat-down she was getting. She was clueless, not corrupt.

Around New Year's, Ruth left a short, pathetic message on our voice mail: "Just checking in, wanting you guys to know we missed you and love you." Three weeks had passed since her shattered sons had fled the penthouse that fateful morning, and only now did she wonder how they might be doing? I swallowed my resentment and sat down to write her a quick e-mail in response, with Mark's tacit approval.

The lawyers have given us strict instructions to have no con-
tact with you at this time. However, I do feel it's important for you
to know that we love you very much and there is never a moment
that goes by when we do not think of you. Everyone is doing
okay . . . but not great. We'll post some new pictures of Audrey
and everyone on the [family] website for you to see. I can't wait
for this mess to settle and . . . we can see you again. It's been very
hard not having you in our life. Please remember that we love you.

She wrote back the next morning, grateful to have the door opened even that little crack.

By the end of January 2009, the press had decamped from our block, and Mark was no longer tied up all day with the attorneys. He had offered his full cooperation to the various agencies now investigating Madoff Securities, and the SEC and FBI had finished debriefing him in a single meeting. Maybe we were turning the corner and would have our lives back soon.

For the first time since the news broke, we spent several days at a stretch without a new bomb dropping. We decided to step out one afternoon to grab some lunch in our neighborhood. When we returned home, the doorman handed us a thick manila envelope. "Oh, God, look at this." Mark showed me. It bore Ruth's unmistakable handwriting, with no return address. We went upstairs, where my mom was watching Audrey. Mark slipped into our glass-walled office to open the envelope privately. Watching warily from the living room,

I saw him put his head in his hands and begin to sob. I ran into the room.

"What is it?" I asked.

"It's all my father's watches." He cried uncontrollably for the first time since Bernie's arrest. Mark held up the open envelope. "Look what you got," he said.

I reached in and felt paper towels wrapped around something heavy. I pulled it out and unwrapped it, revealing a massive rope of diamonds. I remembered telling Ruth how much I loved that necklace. It was stunning, and it had to be worth a fortune. She had worn it to my wedding. Knowing they were about to forfeit everything they owned, the Madoffs clearly wanted their children to have some heirlooms. Optically, though, it couldn't look any worse. And their clumsy gesture could have put us in legal jeopardy, since their assets had been frozen since Bernie's arrest. They were circumventing a court order and putting us smack in the middle of their deceit. Again.

"We've gotta get this stuff out of here," I told Mark. We took the envelope of tainted treasures straight to our attorney's office and handed them over with instructions that they be turned over immediately to federal authorities. The gifts were photographed and itemized first. I was about to throw the paper towels and tissue from the envelope into the lawyer's wastepaper basket when I felt something hard and heavy, like a rock. I unraveled another piece of tissue and found, sure enough, a rock: an enormous emerald ring. Mark picked it up off the table. "My mother always loved this ring so . . ." he murmured sadly. I secretly relished a moment of peculiar pride that Ruth had chosen to honor me with the two pieces I knew were her most prized possessions, even though I would clearly never see them again, much less wear them.

More watches, plus a pair of hideous mink mittens for me—they resembled grizzly bear paws—were sent in a separate Hanukkah package. We found a note tucked in with the diamonds and watches.

> *Dear Mark + Andy, If you can bear to keep these watches, they are given with my love. If not, give them to someone who might. Love, Dad.*

The two handwritten lines on Bernie's embossed stationery were the first Mark had heard from his father since his confession. His only apology had come in mid-January, on an eerily dark and snowy evening, when a text message popped up on Mark's BlackBerry:

> *I'm sorry for all the pain I've caused you. I love you. Love, Dad.*

Bernie never texted or e-mailed. His simple message was both sad and ominous, and we feared that it might be a suicide note. Mark immediately called his attorney, and the U.S. marshals already keeping watch outside of Bernie's building were alerted. They rushed upstairs to find Bernie perfectly calm and lucid.

Mark was constantly worried that we would get a four a.m. knock on the door someday and be put out on the street, all our belongings seized. Within one week of Bernie's arrest, the government had established a monthly spending limit for our basic living expenses, and kept close tabs on our bank balances; we were to turn in regular accounts of every dime we had spent. Mark had even had to seek permission to pay his child support. Our assets were monitored continually while the investigation plodded forward and the inevitable civil suits naming Mark among the defendants were sorted out. Our bank accounts kept being frozen because of the Madoff name (bank employees would see our name in their administrative systems and put an automatic hold on our accounts as a precaution; we would then have to have lawyers and government regulators call to confirm that our accounts weren't under investigation). It was another unpredictable and unnecessary hassle that popped up often for the first few months after Bernie's arrest, and with legal fees to pay and civil suits in the works, our financial situation was precarious.

When I went to BuyBuy Baby to finish shopping for the baby's nursery, I was humiliated when my credit card was abruptly declined. I called Mark, who hurried uptown with a couple of hundred dollars in cash to pay for the bottles, diapers, and such. "I'm so sorry," he kept saying, which only made me more upset. He had done nothing wrong! He had exposed the Ponzi scheme. He had cut off his father forever. He was jobless and unemployable, his mere name synonymous with the most despicable financial crime ever perpetrated. Why were we being made to feel like criminals for buying diapers for a newborn?

When I went for an ultrasound in early February, I got a bit of a mood-boost: The doctor was worried enough about my stress level to suggest inducing labor a couple of weeks early. The baby was already huge. First I would have to undergo another amnio—at thirty-eight weeks—to prove that the baby's lungs were mature enough, but I readily agreed. The needle was long and thick as a straw, and I could feel it puncturing every single layer of tissue as it went deeper into my belly. Mark turned his head away. The pain was horrible, but the news was good: We could choose a birth date in mid-February. We chose Valentine's Day. As the date approached, I got a call from the obstetrician: Valentine's Day was a Saturday, and the hospital wouldn't agree to an elective induction since they were already short-staffed on weekends. I would have to go in the twelfth and have the baby on Friday the thirteenth, or just wait for him to choose his own birthday.

"You promised me a Cupid and now it's going to be a Jason," I joked, thinking of the hockey-masked villain in the *Friday the 13th* movies.

I arrived at Mount Sinai Hospital at nine p.m. on the twelfth, and a resident hooked me up to a fetal monitor.

"Did you feel that?" he asked.

"No," I said, then noted off-handedly that my stomach sort of hurt. "But I think it's just stress."

"That was a contraction," the resident replied. He went off to call my obstetrician. There would be no inducing; I was already in labor.

Mark had brought his Kindle and some of the miniature bottles of

Scotch I had put in his Christmas stocking that year. I had piles of magazines, and *Grey's Anatomy* was on TV. *What a perfect night,* I thought contentedly as we settled in. The residents kept checking, but my cervix had apparently settled in for the night, too. By midnight, it was still stubbornly undilated.

"We're going to have to put a Foley bulb in," I was told. The procedure the resident then explained sounded like something out of *Medieval Torture for Dummies.* An anesthesiologist was paged to come give me an epidural. No one showed up.

"Look," the resident said, "I spoke with your doctor, and he said this has to be done now."

The pain was beyond anything I had ever felt or even imagined.

"I'm going home," I sobbed.

The chief resident appeared. She was blond and cheerful and named Christy, with perfectly manicured black fingernails that I wasn't sure I wanted anywhere near the parts of my body involved in this particular procedure. I could go home if I really wanted to, she said, but why not just give this another try? She would do it herself this time. "C'mon, Steph, just try it," Mark urged.

I reluctantly agreed. The anesthesiologist appeared just as the pain started again, and I got my promised epidural.

"Mark, I don't feel well," I mumbled before turning first white, then blue. A shot of epinephrine brought me to.

They let the epidural wear off and I went from being numb to sheer agony. I was terrified to push. My doctor shouted encouragement at me. Mark was hovering near my face, but remembering that he had bolted during Audrey's delivery, the doctor made me hold my own legs this time.

When Nicholas Henry Madoff finally emerged, I looked for Mark, but Daddy had done the disappearing act again.

"I went behind the curtain because I was crying hysterically and didn't want everyone thinking I was a freak," he sheepishly admitted when he reappeared. Mark held his new son, tears still streaming down his face.

"I just can't believe my parents aren't here to share this," he said sadly.

The Madoffs learned of their grandson's birth via our lawyers. They sent congratulations back via theirs.

A few weeks later, the day after Mark's forty-fifth birthday, Bernie was back in court again to formally plead guilty to the eleven counts lodged against him. In a voice reporters would later describe as devoid of emotion, he expressed remorse and insisted he had acted alone. The judge declared him a flight risk and ordered his bail revoked. He was handcuffed and led away to the city jail to await sentencing.

Mark and I were both worried sick about his mother; she had never been alone her entire life. Behind the puppeteers' backs, I began e-mailing Ruth again, telling her what the kids were up to, sending photos and our love.

I'm so isolated here, she responded. *I'm aching for news of you all.*

In late April, our lawyers gave the green light for me to communicate with her about the grandchildren, and by May we were allowed to arrange for her to come visit the kids and me. Mark wasn't ready to see his mother yet, and the lawyers didn't like the idea, either. I invited Ruth to come on a Tuesday while Mark was in Greenwich visiting Kate and Daniel. I was a nervous wreck and felt my eyes well up with tears when the doorman buzzed to say she was on her way up. When I opened the door, she made a beeline straight for Audrey's room, no hug for me, and spent the afternoon blowing bubbles and playing with her, with a brief interlude to hold baby Nick for the first time. She looked her usual casually fashionable self in designer jeans, but she seemed beat-up, desperately trying to hold it together. I found her sobbing quietly as she gave Audrey her bath. I wrapped her in a hug. Somehow, the words we couldn't find to say to each other in that moment found their way into the e-mails we exchanged later that night.

Please don't feel that today was the only day you could come and visit, I told her. *You are welcome any time . . . and I really mean that. I am here for you. I am sure it was a difficult day for you, but with time it will get easier . . . and one day we will have a normal family again. We just have to find a "new" normal. I love you.*

She answered me a few hours later:

After I recovered a little from seeing you all after so long and missing you all so much, I did feel better . . . I hope you are right

when you say we will be back to a certain kind of normal. Do you
think it is really possible? I dream of such a day. Love, Ruth.

I was dreaming of the future, too. I wanted us to shed everything, go somewhere far from the city and just start fresh. "Let's go to Jackson Hole, just rent someplace for a year," I urged Mark. We had taken family vacations there twice. Bernie had never ventured off the bunny slope and skied with a fat cigar in his mouth. It was hilarious at the time, and if a place was going to conjure any images of Bernie for me, I preferred one where he looked like an idiot. Wyoming was big enough and empty enough to allow us some freedom to live our lives quietly until everything settled down.

Mark immediately nixed the idea. He couldn't be that far away from Kate and Daniel. I refused to let go of my escape fantasy, though, and simply plugged a new zip code into my Internet real-estate searches. We could relocate to Greenwich instead. It would be ideal: Mark would be closer to his older kids, but still within commuting distance of the city, so he could keep looking for work. I would become a suburban mom until fall, when I planned to start classes toward my child life degree. Enrolling in school filled me again with a wonderful sense of possibility. I would be doing something, committing myself to moving forward.

Mark was still paralyzed, though, and I didn't realize at first how much he silently resented my plans. Every time I showed him a house that looked promising, he was noncommittal. Moving permanently

into the house Mark bought before we were married didn't feel right—
I wanted to start over, together. The courts had yet to decide whether
the compensation Mark earned over the years he worked for his father
was untainted by Bernie's criminal conduct.

Bernie's ability to compartmentalize baffles me most when I remember him enjoying lunch on the deck of our home in Nantucket
and watching his grandkids play in the pool, knowing all along that
summer that his house of cards was about to topple, bringing us all
down with him. But Bernie had had his own optics to maintain for
decades, and his family's life was his biggest illusion. "Was he living
vicariously through our happiness?" I asked Mark. We decided to
spend one last summer in the magical place where we had assumed we
would grow old together. Bernie was due to be sentenced that June,
and we wanted to be out of the city when it happened.

When we arrived on Nantucket, some friends who lived there
year-round were waiting to greet us in the driveway. I fell into their
arms and started sobbing. It just felt so good to be there again. Mark
filled his lungs with the sharp, purgative smell of low tide. On June
26, 2009, the day Bernie was sentenced, we went out to dinner with
our friends to celebrate.

"Congratulations, buddy, you made it," one of our friends toasted
Mark.

"We survived," I said, repeating it for good measure. "We survived."

That afternoon, Mark had deliberately stayed down on the beach, fishing for shark, until the appointed hour. I watched the news for us both. The judge noted that not a single person—even from his own family—had written a letter in support of Bernie.

"What'd he get?" Mark asked when he came inside.

"One hundred and fifty years," I reported. He would be spending it as Inmate Number 61727054 at the medium-security Federal Correctional Complex in rural Butner, North Carolina.

Bernie Madoff was gone for good.

What I didn't realize was that Mark Madoff was, too.

five

THE BOOK OF RUTH

The perfect family proved to be, like everything else revolving around Bernie, pure illusion. The little cracks I noticed in that smooth, shiny surface long before the scandal turned fissures into canyons, marooning each Madoff on a different cliff's edge. How each member of this family coped, or didn't, in the face of disaster would be fascinating, I suppose, for some social scientist looking from the outside in. But from the inside looking out it was maddening and, at the end of the day, achingly sad.

Maybe it's a result of being raised by a lawyer, but I prefer to face trouble head-on and push past it. And if someone I love has been wronged by anyone, my loyalties are never ambiguous. The Madoffs were the complete opposite; what I had initially presumed to be a lack of conflict within their ranks was actually an inability to deal with it. The result was a sort of collective emotional paralysis. Bernie, the patriarch, was the weakest of them all, yet he cultivated a public image as a financial genius, one that gave him an undeniable aura of authority. His family, like his unsuspecting investors, held him in awe. People mistook his reserve for intellect, though I can't remember ever seeing Bernie scan a newspaper or read a book, as Ruth was wont to do; TV and movies were his medium. It took me years to figure out that my father-in-law's pleasant veneer was just that, and only that. The façade was highly polished, but whatever substance there once might have been behind it had long since dried and crumbled by the time I knew him. That said, it was easy to like Bernie and get along with him, to enjoy his company. You just had to accept that you weren't ever going to genuinely connect with him on anything beyond a superficial level. You might laugh at him, but never with him, over his little idiosyncrasies.

Though Mark loved and admired Bernie greatly, I never heard— or heard of—a meaningful conversation between father and son. On the rare occasions when some deeper feeling nudged its way to the surface, Bernie panicked and shut down altogether. When Mark was fourteen, I learned in a jailhouse letter from Bernie, he had discovered a lump on his groin one Friday afternoon while the family was getting ready to leave on a boat trip from Montauk to Maine. A doctor friend on the dock in Long Island took one look and told Ruth and Bernie to get their son to his pediatrician right away. Fearing Hodgkin's disease, the pediatrician arranged for Mark to undergo a biopsy that

Monday at the hospital. *My reaction was to crawl into bed that Friday afternoon and sleep straight through until Monday morning,* Bernie recounted.

This story was intended to show me what a caring, devoted father Bernie had been, but it still reinforces my suspicion about just how deep this man's narcissism ran, how well rehearsed he was in the cold art of abandonment. In his mind, Mark's health scare was all about what a terrible ordeal it was for Bernie. Ruth, Mark, and Andy are conveniently forgotten and left to cope on their own with the scary three-day wait. The biopsy came back clean. Mark was fine, and the swelling turned out to be just an infection. Decades later, Bernie would hit the off switch again when Andy was diagnosed with lymphoma. Bernie exhibited those same symptoms of an impending zone-out in the weeks leading up to the exposure and collapse of his Ponzi scheme. His soul simply lacked the square footage for ego and emotion to comfortably coexist.

I was shocked, and terribly hurt for Mark, by Bernie's lack of concern for his son after Mark had stormed out of his parents' penthouse the morning his father confessed. Bernie didn't call out or run after him, nor did he try to telephone, visit, or reach out to his wounded son following the stunning confrontation. Mark's legal team had advised him, needlessly, not to have any contact with Bernie or Ruth while the federal investigation moved forward. It's safe to assume that Bernie's lawyers issued a similar no-contact edict. But Bernie had promptly admitted his guilt to the FBI agents who arrested him, and he surely knew from the beginning that he would no doubt die in prison. So what did he really have to lose, I had to wonder, if he chose to ignore the lawyers and answer to some deeper, father's instinct? The only answer I could come up with: There was nothing deeper.

Although the media would miscast her as a Stepford wife, Ruth, truth be told, was far more complex and intriguing than her childhood sweetheart. Mark and I initially worried that his parents might carry out some kind of suicide pact before Bernie was sent away, but Ruth proved to be an extraordinary survivor. She also had an uncanny ability to compartmentalize, coupled with a talent for playing two sides against the middle in any scenario. She knew how to subtly manipulate people to get what she needed, and she wasn't above doing it for pure sport, either. At the last family Thanksgiving dinner I had hosted, just before Bernie's arrest, I was horrified to discover that Ruth had quietly invited her son Andy's estranged wife, Debbie, to my get-together, knowing full well that Andy would most likely be bringing his new live-in girlfriend, Catherine Hooper. I was able to warn Debbie off in time, and I knew better than to even try to ask Ruth what she had been thinking. Her defense when she was caught out in these little pocket dramas was to act nonchalant; if it didn't make any difference to her, it shouldn't to anyone else, either. Her casual indifference gave her power. When I look back now, I can see how Ruth's constant little digs and comments used to feed my animosity toward Mark's ex-wife, Susan, as much as anything Susan herself did or said. Ruth loved to build you up, and then not so much knock you down as flick you aside.

"Oh my God, I can't figure out what to get Kate and Daniel for Hanukkah," Ruth once called me up to moan. "What are you doing?

You always give the best gifts." I felt a surge of gratitude and pride that my mother-in-law had noticed how much thought I put into choosing presents for my family and friends. "I'm such a dope," Ruth went on, "I don't know what to do! Do you have any ideas?" Before I could make any useful suggestions, Ruth fired her sharpest arrow straight into my Achilles' heel. "Oh, you know what? Forget it, I'll just call Susan!" Now you count, now you don't.

For nearly a year following Bernie's confession, however, I felt closer to Ruth than I ever had. I pitied her and was genuinely frightened for her. Her loyalty to Bernie was hard to stomach, but I was willing to give her the benefit of the doubt and view it as a form of denial that would wear off once she was faced with the reality of her husband's being locked up for good. Bernie had always been her validation. Despite her brash Queens exterior, Ruth could be surprisingly insecure. Looks were extremely important to her. She was obsessed with staying thin and looking younger than her sixty-something peers, and she worked hard at it. Her fashion sense was youthful enough to make Andy's girlfriend, who was nearly thirty years her junior, exclaim out loud how excited she was that they wore the same size, so she could claim any Ruth castoffs. For the most part, though, Ruth's look was firmly rooted in the 1980s, and she was averse to change. Navy eyeliner rimmed her beautiful blue eyes, and pancake foundation created a monotone complexion. She wore berry-pink lipstick outlined with a brick-colored lip liner, and her frosted blond hair in a simple chin-length bob. She would ask where I had my hair done, make an appointment, and try something slightly different, only to quickly revert to what was familiar. At my wedding, I was thrilled when my close friend Nei, a makeup artist, offered his services as a gift. Ruth asked him to do her face, too, and Nei obliged with his signature understated style. Ruth looked fresh and pretty. She headed off to her room to change into her pewter sheath and diamond-rope necklace. When she reappeared at the ceremony, Nei was hurt to see that she had wiped everything off and whipped out the pageant-queen pancake and lip liner again.

Despite her preferences at the makeup counter, Ruth could easily pass for a woman ten years younger. Her two face-lifts had been expertly done, and she aggressively fought any wrinkles with fillers, laser treatments, and Botox. Veneers gave her a perfect smile, and you were more likely to see her laughing than not, before her world came crashing in.

Ruth worked out with a personal trainer a few times a week, and when it came to dieting, her self-discipline was unmatched. A carb never touched her lips. Even on vacations, I never saw her eat so much as a single dinner roll, slice of toast, or even cracker with cheese. She would rinse the mayo off the coleslaw when I bought a tub to go with a roast chicken for a casual family lunch—if she wasn't going to have it, I guess no one was—and when we occasionally made the mistake of tossing out the chicken carcass after Mark had carved it and put the meat on a serving platter, Ruth would dig through the trash to retrieve it. The carcass was her favorite part. She would put the skeletal remains on a plate in front of her and happily nibble and suck away at the bones. While Bernie scarfed down his favorite cherry pie for dessert, Ruth permitted herself only frozen chocolate-dipped bananas from John's Drive-In in Montauk. Her freezer there was always full of them. She also let me in on her secret trick for portion control at restaurants: Once she had eaten the amount of lean protein she considered reasonable, she would dump a ghastly amount of salt over whatever was left on her plate to keep herself from overeating. Wine was her only real indulgence; Bernie's adherence to Diet Coke or iced tea didn't mean she wasn't going to enjoy a few glasses of Sauvignon Blanc. If he disapproved, he never showed it.

The only time I heard any of Ruth's backstory before 2008 was once while I was visiting the Madoffs at their home in Palm Beach, and Ruth's older sister, Joan, who lived nearby in Boca Raton, came over to spend the afternoon with us in Ruth's cabana at the Breakers Hotel. I started asking questions about their upbringing in Far Rockaway. The two daughters of Saul and Sara Alpern had discovered only after their mother's death that they may have been illegitimate; Sara, it seemed, had been married before, but never legally divorced her first husband. Ruth and Joan said they still hadn't figured out exactly what had—or hadn't—happened.

Though media accounts would describe Ruth as growing up more solidly middle-class than Bernie and his family, Ruth and Joan described themselves as relatively poor. Ruth, however, proved resourceful from an early age. "I made my own clothes," she confided with a measure of pride. Petite and bubbly, Ruth was just thirteen when she and Bernie spotted each other in the basement rec room where a friend with a jukebox was throwing a party. Bernie was sixteen, a junior in high school; Ruth had just graduated from eighth grade. "He came with a date," Ruth recounted with a devilish smile, "but he left with me." She married him when she was eighteen, just two months before her new husband officially launched Bernard L. Madoff Investment Securities.

A razor-sharp wit had always been Ruth's suit of armor, and she clearly relied on it (as well as the Wellbutrin that she confided her therapist had prescribed) to endure the very public humiliation her husband caused us all. Returning from her first visit to the Metropolitan Correctional Center to see Bernie behind bars, Ruth was cracking jokes about hanging with all the women waiting to see their men in jail—just another well-groomed Park Avenue grandma chilling with her new gangbanger girlfriends. Ruth even spent her sixty-eighth birthday at the jail, describing it merely as "surreal."

Ruth broke her six-month public silence about the case only after a federal judge denounced Bernie's crimes as "extraordinarily evil" and meted out his 150-year sentence. Ruth wasn't in the courtroom, but sent me an e-mail saying she felt *a little ill. I was prepared for what was to be a lifelong sentence, but this is making me really sick. All I really cared about is whether he would be sent to a maximum security and it might be a possibility with this length sentence besides the total shame of it all. I feared this but I didn't think it would happen.*

She prepared a statement for the media. She wrote it herself, re-drafting the ending, by her own account, at least ten times. She asked me to review it before releasing it. I urged her to drop the final paragraph, lest she torpedo any chance she had of rebuilding her own public image.

Many wonder if I can still love a man who did this and I understand that, she had written. *But this is the man, for better or for worse, whom I married forty-nine years ago. How does one discard forty-nine years of a lifetime? My connection to him has been forged through the years and I cannot abandon him.*

After his sentencing, a prison physical revealed high levels of prostate-specific antigens in Bernie's blood, which prompted Ruth to gleefully speculate that health issues might guarantee her beloved placement in a medium-security prison.

Prostate cancer, good news! she joked darkly in an e-mail.

I hate to say it, but it is probably the best thing that could happen to him, I answered, hastening to add that a high PSA didn't necessarily mean cancer, anyway.

At least Bernie had a place to stay, which is more than he left his loyal wife. All four Madoff homes and their contents were being auctioned, with proceeds going to the victims' fund. U.S. marshals sold off everything from diamonds to dust mops. Even Bernie's boxer shorts would go on the block, fetching a couple of hundred dollars. Some questionable hype was used to advertise certain items in the sales catalog: A 10.5 karat emerald-cut diamond valued at $550,000 and described as Ruth's "engagement ring" was a mystery to me, for example. I'd never seen it before, and there's no way Bernie, at twenty-two, could have purchased it for his teenaged fiancée. Ruth usually sported a simple gold or platinum band, and favored a gorgeous emerald ring when she was dressing up for a special event—the same one she had wrapped in a wad of tissue and mailed to us following Bernie's arrest.

A week before she was forced out of the penthouse she and Bernie had called home for nearly twenty-five years, Ruth still wasn't sure what possessions were considered hers and what was going to be confiscated. *I don't know what I can take,* she fretted. *They're going to take all the furniture, my good clothes, shoes, purses, etc., and I'll have to buy back anything of value that I want to take. I don't even know if I can take my computer or even one TV set.* All Madoff assets were frozen, and though she had not been criminally charged, Ruth was still forced to report any expenditure over $100 to the court-appointed trustees. On the day she was forced to vacate the penthouse with the few boxes of basic necessities she was allowed to keep, Ruth hid in the trunk of a car and had her building superintendent drive her away so she wouldn't have to face the media waiting outside to witness her humiliating eviction. She had tried in vain to hold on to $69 million in assets her lawyers claimed were unrelated to the fraud, and ended up settling for $2.5 million, which immediately became the target of civil lawsuits from investors who had been defrauded.

Ruth spent the summer with relatives in Long Island and Florida, then scoured the city for a decent one- or two-bedroom apartment to rent that fall, but leases fell through as soon as landlords discovered the identity of their prospective tenant. I went with her and her broker to look at some places. We would trek up four flights of stairs to some

dingy apartment with a hot plate instead of a stove and curtains droop-
ing off a broken rod, and she would shake her head in disgust and
disbelief at how much money even a dump commanded in Manhattan.
"I just can't," she would say. "It's so depressing." There was one
studio with a ladder leading to a sleeping loft that might have been
suitable for a college kid, but was hardly feasible for a woman ap-
proaching seventy, and another that Ruth rejected because there was
no counter space for her makeup mirror in the tiny bathroom.

I urged her to look downtown so she could be closer to us, though
Mark later admitted to me that he wasn't too keen on that idea. She
was such a target for paparazzi, and so widely recognized by then, that
he worried about her picking Audrey up from school or taking her to
a neighborhood park. It didn't matter, anyway; no landlord downtown was willing to accept Ruth's application, either. There was no
way she was going to pass anyone's background check. "I'm being
blackballed by the New York Jewish real-estate community," she
wailed. "Bernie had a lot of important real-estate people that were
hurt, and they put the word out, *Don't rent to Ruth Madoff.* And no
one will. I'm hanging by a thread here."

Desperate to shake the tabloid vultures who stalked her, Ruth initially tried to disguise herself with a brown pageboy wig with girlish
bangs, which she found at a Hasidic yard sale in Long Island. She sent
us a photo her sister had taken of her wearing it, looking for all the
world like an aged and forgotten Spice Girl. Later attempts to dye her
hair brown or red were less ridiculous. Once her maiden name became
known and was no longer a reliable alias, Ruth chose a new one: Jane

Green. That she named herself after the color of money was not an irony lost on me, but who knows whether she was trying to be funny or just didn't think first.

Jane Green became a nomad dependent on the charity of others, including those her husband had ruined. For months on end, Ruth bounced between the homes of her sister, a niece, and the few friends who hadn't shunned her. She had once boasted a tight circle of four girlfriends who did everything together, including an African safari, but Bernie had cleaned out those couples, too. I had met and greatly enjoyed Ruth's lively little posse, and was surprised and touched one afternoon when I answered my phone to hear one of them calling "just to check in on you." An instant later, the woman was screaming at me: "We have nothing! We're having to split roast chicken from Publix for dinner. My granddaughters are going to public school and I'm worried sick they'll be bullied. My husband and I are old. We can't get jobs. We got nothing. At least you and Mark are young and have the rest of your life ahead of you!" I hung up, wondering whether Ruth was getting a daily dose of the same vitriol. She hadn't changed her cell phone number since the arrest.

For Mark and me, the Bernie backlash was more subtle, but still hurtful. I found myself excluded from the bridal party of one of my old Breakfast Club friends, and passed over as godmother by another. People who had once bragged about knowing a Madoff son and daughter-in-law suddenly were embarrassed to acknowledge us. I learned quickly who my real friends were, and held them close. I was going to need them more than ever to get through what was yet to come. My parents had been ripped off by Bernie, but fortunately, none of my friends had been victimized.

I have to be in hiding wherever I am, and it's intolerable, Ruth wrote me from her sister's in Boca Raton, where Joan and her husband stayed afloat by driving an airport shuttle cab after their retirement nest egg had been wiped out by Bernie. *I can't use my name anywhere and it all becomes so complicated with airplane travel, car rental, etc.* She talked about legally changing her name once things quieted down. (Divorcing Bernie, however, was never mentioned.)

Although Mark and I never experienced the ostracism Ruth did, I was eager to shed the Madoff name by then. Mark fully supported the decision and planned to do the same as soon as his lawyers gave the go-ahead. We liked trying on different possibilities. Mark and our friend Joe were big fans of *Dexter,* the TV drama about a forensic analyst who moonlights as a serial killer targeting murderers. "Oh, hey," Mark casually mentioned while watching the show one night, "Joe and I were talking and thought: 'Stephanie Morgan.'"

"That sounds good," I agreed, thinking I'd much rather bear the surname of a fictional serial killer than a real-life con artist.

"Well, sit with it a little while," Mark suggested. I did, for several months, then had my attorney file the sealed documents requesting the name change for myself, Audrey, and Nicholas. It was a saddening move: Mark and I were both old-fashioned about a wife taking her husband's name, and I had been so proud to be Mrs. Mark Madoff. I loved him and wanted the world to know I belonged to him. Even though we were in full agreement about the change and Mark intended to follow suit, it still felt as if we were losing part of our identity as a couple. I just wished I could change my birthday, as well; I share the date with Bernie.

The afternoon my petition was filed, I was killing time before going to a friend's house for dinner when Mark texted me: *Name was leaked, NY Post outside building.* The order, I learned later, had been stolen off the judge's desk while the judge was at a doctor's appointment. The judge called my attorney, appalled and apologetic, and told me to pick a new name. He would take the paperwork home and hand-carry it to chambers the next morning. I hastily settled on Mack, which combined my husband's first initial with the airport code for our favorite place, Nantucket.

"That's genius!" Mark approved. "I love it." I felt a twinge of guilt when I realized that he would someday have to become Mark Mack, which sounded like a comic-strip detective, but I knew he would be as relieved as I was to no longer carry the most shameful name in America. I couldn't even stand to see it on old prescription bottles in my medicine cabinet, or have a salesclerk notice it on my credit card. Mark and I had both cringed when we had to wear name-tags while mingling with other parents and teachers at preschool open houses while looking for a place to enroll Audrey just months after Bernie's arrest. Thank God everyone was gracious enough not to ask us if we were *those* Madoffs.

Our worst incident was probably the insensitive phone call we got from the director of Pinecliffe, the summer camp Kate had attended in Maine for several years. To accommodate divorced parents, the

TOP LEFT: *Mark and me in Key West, Florida, December 2002. This was one of our first trips away together.* TOP RIGHT: *Same fishing trip, at Little Palm Island.* BOTTOM LEFT: *Visiting Mark at his house in Greenwich, Connecticut, spring 2003.* BOTTOM RIGHT: *East River fishing, September 2004. I was determined to always be the fun-loving good sport Mark wanted in his life.* BELOW: *The place where we both truly felt relaxed, St. Barths, spring 2003.*

TOP LEFT: *My thirtieth birthday party turned into an engagement party, April 2004.* TOP RIGHT: *The morn of our wedding, Nantucket, October 23, 2004.*

BOTTOM LEFT: *The wedding ceremony. Left to right: Mark's daughter Kate; my brother, Rob; me; Mark; ar Mark's son Daniel.* BOTTOM RIGHT: *Our reception was one fantastic party.*

Saying "I do." A truly happy moment.

Mr. and Mrs. Mark Madoff.
Narciso's dress was perfection.

Bernie and Ruth, my new in-laws.

An autumn-themed cake to go with our Thanksgiving dinner.

Bernie and me.

Ruth and Bernie in a celebratory mood.

The first stop on our honeymoon,
North Island, Seychelles.

Married bliss, fishing in Key West, 2005.

TOP LEFT: *One of Bernie's visits to feed Audrey a bottle in the middle of a working day. This image stirs complicated feelings in me, as I try to reconcile the doting grandfather and the financial schemer as one and the same.* TOP RIGHT: *Bernie, Ruth, Audrey, and me, vacationing in the south of France, June 2007.* BOTTOM LEFT: *Audrey with her grandparents on* Bull, *Bernie's yacht in the south of France.* BOTTOM RIGHT: *Mother and daughter. I had so much fun on this trip.*

Ruth, Audrey, and Bernie, New York City, 2007.

The Madoff ladies. Top to bottom: Ruth, me, Kate, and Audrey in New York City, fall 2007.

Mark and Grouper.

Audrey and Mark, Nantucket, summer 2007.

Mark's forty-fourth birthday, March 2008.

Audrey and Mark, Hotel du Cap, Antibes.

Bernie sitting on the deck of our
new house in Nantucket, summer 2008.

Mark and Audrey on summer vacation
in Nantucket, 2008.

Ruth and Bernie at Audrey's second
birthday party, about ten days before
Bernie's confession, November 2008.

Mark and Audrey, pumpkin-picking, fall 2008.

Andy, Mark, and my brother, Rob,
also at Audrey's birthday party.

TOP LEFT: *Bernie and my stepfather, Marty, at Audrey's party. Marty had just recently given Bernie a sizable portion of his retirement savings to invest.* TOP RIGHT: *Bernie knew at this point that his lies were coming back to haunt him. It's astounding he was able to hold himself together like he did that day.* LEFT: *Mark and me in Nantucket the first week of December 2008, during the Christmas Stroll, which is one of my favorite events of the year. I was seven months pregnant with Nicholas.* BELOW: *Mark and Audrey choosing the Christmas tree, December 7, 2008. Our holiday excitement was flattened just days later, when Bernie confessed.*

Mark and Audrey, just weeks after Bernie's arrest, December 2008. Mark was destroyed by his father's confession, though we both tried hard to keep our trauma hidden from the kids.

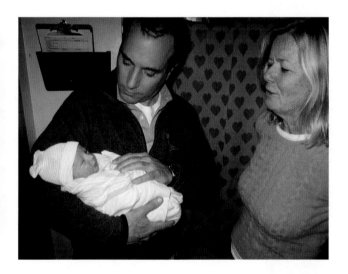

Nicholas was born February 13, 2009. Proud dad Mark with my mother, Pinks.

Nick, Mark, and Audrey. It seemed at this point there was hope for rebuilding our happy family life again.

Father and son.

OPPOSITE PAGE, TOP LEFT: *Family portraits, early 2010. After a disastrous few months, Mark seemed genu-nely to be in a better place.* TOP RIGHT: *Greenwich, October 2009. Mark was recently home from the hospital, nd though it was a sad time, he valued more than ever the good things in his life rather than what had been aken away from him.* MIDDLE LEFT: *Halloween 2009. I absolutely loved getting the kids dressed up and xcited for any holiday.* MIDDLE RIGHT: *Nick's first birthday, New York City, February 2010. Mark and I vere determined to celebrate happy family moments, though our stress shows.* BOTTOM LEFT: *Mark, Nick, nd me. Mark's proud expression breaks my heart when I look at this picture.* BOTTOM RIGHT: *Left to right: Nick, Kate, Daniel, me, Mark, and Audrey.*

TOP LEFT: *Montauk, Summer 2010.* TOP RIGHT: *One of our last photos, and our last weekend together a* *a family, at the Montauk lighthouse, post-Thanksgiving weekend 2010.* BOTTOM LEFT: *Audrey's fourt* *birthday. Mark and I were in a good place as a couple, and Mark was happy about and inspired by hi* *new job.* BOTTOM RIGHT: *Nick's second birthday, 2011.*

Audrey and Nick both draw pictures for their dad,
and we hang them in the apartment windows so he can see them from the sky.

Mark in St. Barths, one of the places he felt happiest, February 2006.
I keep this photo on my nightstand.

In Nantucket, March 2011.
It would have been Mark's forty-seventh birthday.

camp sets aside two visiting days per season. The mother of another camper with family ties to the New York Mets—a major investor in Bernie's fraudulent fund—had demanded that we not show up on the same day she was visiting her daughter. I was sickened at the thought that poor Kate might have been subjected to any trickle-down cruelty, but she seemed fine when we went to visit. Around us, the kids never brought up Papa Bernie and what he had done.

Even with supportive friends, though, there was always a certain undercurrent of embarrassment for us. We could be out to dinner with other couples, having a good time, but I always wondered afterward whether the conversation shifted once we left the table. *Do you think they knew? Are they going to lose their apartment? Is everything they own basically stolen?*

But the most difficult relationship of all to navigate was the one between Mark and his mother. Mark never asked for any details about my post-arrest relationship with Ruth, and while he seemed grateful that I was trying to look after her, he still struggled to work through his own conflicted feelings. His lawyers' initial advice to keep his distance gave him the perfect excuse to avoid the difficult task of deciding whether his relationship with Ruth could be salvaged. He didn't flat-out hate her the way he did Bernie, but from the beginning, he found her continued devotion to a man who had caused so much pain to so many—most of all, to his own family—infuriating. His dismay deepened when she continued to hold fast to her destructive marriage even after Bernie had been transferred to North Carolina to spend the rest of his life locked up. She refused to see what she was doing to her sons even when old friends spelled it out, as Bernie's longtime secretary did for a *Vanity Fair* reporter.

Eleanor says that I gave up my children to see Bernie, Ruth complained to me in an e-mail when the magazine piece appeared. *It's not one or the other,* she insisted, though her older son, at least, had made it crystal clear to her that it was. *I feel so sorry for him,* she added, meaning, of course, Bernie. *He must have suffered so during his life . . . I know he didn't get into this because of greed or to thoughtlessly hurt anyone.* Why he did, then, she didn't explain.

Having cut off their father completely and their mother almost entirely save for brief e-mail exchanges, the Madoff brothers were at odds with each other as well in the middle of the firestorm that still raged around them. Mark and Andy had gone from working side by side every day of their adult lives and spending vacations fishing together to speaking only when they met at the offices of the legal team they shared. Petty grievances festered into deep wounds. Andy's girlfriend, Catherine, invariably seemed to be a factor. He had introduced her to the rest of the family several months before Bernie's arrest, to less-than-enthusiastic reviews. Eager to welcome her into the fold early on, I had met her for coffee at Balthazar, a nearby SoHo restaurant. "I'm curious to know what you think of her," Mark said beforehand.

I came home convinced that we'd clicked and that I had just made a wonderful new friend. "I think she's great," I gushed to Mark. "I liked her a lot."

"Just be careful, Stephanie," he cautioned. "There's something weird about her. Something I just find off." It was unusual for him to sound an alarm like that, but I brushed his concern aside.

Soon enough, though, Mark's instincts were borne out, and we both got the impression that Catherine was trying a little too desperately to muscle her way into the Madoff family, whether it was angling for exclusive use of a company driver or leaping at the chance to join Bernie and Ruth on vacation in the south of France. I secretly envied her confidence and the way she simply claimed the status she wanted, which was something I still wrestled with even several years and one grandchild into my marriage. For Mark, the last straw was when Catherine invited herself along on a guys-only fishing tournament he and Andy had entered with some buddies. Mark threw a fit and she stayed away, but the incident spoiled the trip. My wake-up came seven months before Bernie's arrest, on Mother's Day. We had all gone out for a celebratory dinner the night before—Mark, Audrey, and me, Andy and Catherine, the Madoffs, my parents, and my brother and sister-in-law. I had given Ruth a necklace with a silver macaroni charm from Audrey.

"Thank you for the beautiful flowers," Ruth said when she called the next day.

"I didn't send you flowers," I said, puzzled.

"It says you did on the card," Ruth replied, equally puzzled. She read it to me: *Thought you might need a buttering-up from the women who adore your sons.* Since there were only two sons, and two women, that left only one possible suspect: Andy's girlfriend. Catherine's presumptuousness ticked me off, but I was also mortified by the juvenile message on the card. I would never say something so cheesy, nor would I piggyback onto someone else's gift. If I wanted to send Ruth flowers, I would do so on my own. I sent an e-mail to Catherine, copying Mark and Andy: *It would've been nice if you had told me you were going to send flowers to Ruth from me*, I said. Mark soon called me from the office.

"Stephanie, this Mother's Day thing with the flowers is out of control," he said. "She's saying she didn't send flowers from both of you, just her."

"But your mother read me the card," I protested, recounting the message to him. This was getting ludicrous. It wasn't *The Da Vinci Code*.

Mark went back to Andy, who was now going by "Andrew" at Catherine's behest, and the denials grew even more vehement: The florist must have transcribed the card wrong. By now, unfortunately, Mark's love of TV cop shows and Vince Flynn thrillers was getting the best of him, and he decided to play sleuth. He contacted the florist and got him to forward the e-mail order, which did, in fact, identify Catherine Hooper as the person who had placed it, spelling out the message she wanted on the card. The wording was exactly as Ruth had relayed it to me.

Mark triumphantly confronted Andy with proof of the floral felony. A huge, stupid blowup ensued, and for the first time Mark could remember, a rift formed between the brothers. Andy was deeply hurt and confused. He was in love; why couldn't his brother just be happy for him? Catherine phoned Mark at work, calling him a pathetic loser and telling him to fuck off and stop trying to ruin her relationship. "She was going crazy," he told me, laughing. A month later, she boycotted what would turn out to be the final Madoff party in Montauk and let it be known it was because she felt unwanted. Andy spent the weekend sulking, his anger sucking the oxygen out of the house. He and Mark barely spoke. Ruth and Bernie were upset, exchanging occasional worried looks but making no attempt to mediate. They had never seen this kind of tension between their two boys. "She makes me very nervous," Bernie remarked about Catherine when Andy was out of earshot.

The brothers still saw each other at work every day, but that was pretty much it. After Bernie's arrest, without the daily contact they had had at the office, Mark and Andy grew even further apart, dealing with the family's implosion in their own separate ways. Where there had once been such solidarity, there was now just tension, emptiness, and heartache.

Andy was in the same straits as Mark as a result of their father's crime, though he reacted very differently from how his brother did. At one point, when on the street while picking up dinner from a takeout place, Andy was confronted by an enraged former employee who made a nasty remark about Catherine, who was sitting in the car nearby. Andy punched him.

But Andy didn't seem to be devastated by the relentless scrutiny, and even found ways to exploit the infamous Madoff name in publicizing the disaster-preparedness kits Catherine had begun selling online. Without a job to go to every day at his father's firm, Andy focused on other business ventures that he and Mark had explored apart from Madoff Securities, including their fly-fishing reel company and an alternative-energy enterprise. Andy had encouraged Mark to take a more active role in developing a new product line they envisioned for the fly-fishing business, but Mark had quickly grown bored. It wasn't challenging, and it wasn't filling his days.

Mark by then was uninterested even in the things he used to love, like live theater or working out. Andy had poured himself into his outside pursuits. He became an avid bicyclist and joined a cycling club. He focused more intently on the piano lessons he had taken for years. Mark passed the time by obsessively following every scrap of news and commentary about the Madoff scandal, stewing in his own indignation about its effects on him. When the story of Ruth being evicted from the penthouse broke, with the U.S. Marshals Service holding a lobby news conference to announce that she had "vacated the residence" and "surrendered all personal property" to federal agents, Mark reached out to his mother for the first time in seven months.

I'm sure that today f*cking sucked, he e-mailed her. *However, try and look at it as a new start. I love you.*

Ruth answered back a couple of hours later, describing it as "beyond any humiliation you can imagine." The media, she said, was ruining any chance she might have of making a new life for herself. *I'm pretty numb by now but not numb enough. How did I become the focus of all this.*

That fall, with Bernie gone and nowhere to go herself, Ruth broached the possibility of seeing Mark again for the first time in nearly a year. "I'm still confused about her," Mark told me. He didn't want to hurt her, but he didn't want to see her, either. "Do you think this is okay?" he asked me, showing me the e-mail he had carefully crafted to send her.

Mom, I need you to be patient with us. When I tell you that we are on the edge, I am not kidding, he wrote. *That means individually and as a couple. Unfortunately, the shame of what my father has done has become almost too overwhelming. On top of that, I may be facing bankruptcy and I'm not sure how we will deal with that. Stephanie and I are hunkering down and doing our best. Right now, it's just me and her. Once we get some closure, you and I will work on things and begin rebuilding.*

Tragically, Ruth opted to pitch her tent in the rubble instead.

six

RIPTIDE

What happened to us reminded me of a recurring nightmare I'd had as a little girl. I was with my stepfather, mother, and brother on Marty's boat, which had a big, open back you could fish off of. I was standing there when, out of nowhere, a huge wave appeared and started chasing us, growing bigger and closer as Marty, at the helm, tried heroically to outrace it. The dream was a child's version, I guess, of sailors' stories about freak waves suddenly appearing in the middle of the ocean, rearing a hundred feet high and swallowing large ships whole. Eyewitnesses described the deep trough created by the monster wave before it crested as a hole in the sea.

Exactly how and why rogue waves form is still debated, but they appear unexpectedly from directions counter to prevailing winds and waves, and they loom at least twice the size of surrounding waves. If a ship has the right amount of ballast and is floating at the proper level before the wall of water hits, it can survive a rogue wave and right itself. Survival is a matter of balance.

A love of the sea, with all its mystery and majesty, was something Mark and I had always shared. When we returned to Nantucket just before Bernie was sentenced in the summer of 2009, I was certain that the island would shelter and restore us, that the sharp salt air would scour us of the lingering stench of the Madoff scandal. This place where we had been married, more than any other, defined us as husband and wife. Maybe here Mark would snap out of his funk and allow himself to enjoy life's little pleasures again, like digging for clams with your toes and grilling them for dinner, or watching the dog chase waves.

Learning to surf topped my list of things to try that summer. I tracked down the colorful van that served as headquarters of the Nantucket Island Surf School in the parking lot of Cisco Beach and, three months after giving birth to Nicholas, signed up for lessons. I arrived each day to squeeze into my borrowed wetsuit, eager to paddle out beyond the frothy breakers.

Getting to your feet is the hardest part. I remember straddling the surfboard, legs dangling in the sea, waiting for the current to swell beneath me and carry me, laughing, back to shore. Mark would be waiting there, waving and cheering me on, while the kids played in the sand. As beginners, we were tethered to our loaner boards by ankle leashes, guided by the impossibly healthy, suntanned college kids who made up the faculty of this eclectic summer academy. At thirty-five, I was by far the oldest student. The instructors would offer to tow us out to catch a wave, but I always refused. I wanted to earn my wave. I wanted to feel every muscle burn and every nerve tingle. If I wiped out, I wanted to right myself and fight my way back in. Rescue defeated the purpose of risk.

The wetsuit made me feel snug and secure, insulated from the cold tide and the unseen dangers below and beyond me. I tried not to think about the dusky sharks Mark regularly caught fishing off the beach just below our beloved gray-shingled Nantucket house, or even worse, the great whites that had been spotted a few times that year. Surfing is my happiest memory of that season in Nantucket. It was to be our last. The house would likely be going on the market.

Moving on and reclaiming the joy in life was much harder for Mark, though. Severing all ties to his father had been instantaneous and irrevocable for him, but his relationship with his mother was still at an impasse. Mark had always been something of a mama's boy, much more like his extroverted mother than his rather reserved father. He and Ruth had been close, and Ruth left no doubts that she was proud of her eldest son. When she met my mother for the first time before Mark and I were married, Ruth made a point of quaintly assuring her that "my son is a very honorable man." But when that same quality she so prized in her child proved to be chillingly absent in her husband, Ruth faltered. Six months after Bernie's arrest, Ruth still didn't see that there was no such thing as neutrality in this particular war. Even if she had had no knowledge or suspicion whatsoever of Bernie's crimes, choosing his side after he was exposed seemed both foolish and dangerous. Optically unwise, as the crisis managers would say. To an already unsympathetic public, Ruth looked as if she were tacitly endorsing Bernie's actions.

Mark's own aversion to Bernie ran so deep that he would take detours to avoid driving past his parents' apartment building if we were in midtown Manhattan. Once, when Audrey was invited to a friend's birthday party right across the street from the Madoff penthouse, I cajoled Mark into coming along. I felt guilty as soon as we turned into the block, though; Mark looked absolutely nauseated. He bolted within minutes of arriving.

I knew even at the beginning of our relationship that Mark's personal life could be thoroughly affected by broken relationships. When his first marriage had ended, Mark told me, he had felt so hurt that he had purged himself of any reminders of that union in one fell swoop, tossing all his personal belongings away—watches, clothing, even shoes. He rented an apartment in the city, and on the same day went to Crate & Barrel and bought a new life, simply pointing to the staged displays: "I'll take that bedroom, and that living room."

Bernie's betrayal had triggered a similar purge. Every single picture of him came down in our home, and Mark pitched everything his father had ever given him, down to the last sweater. Bernie had been a shopaholic, especially when it came to clothes. He put Carrie Bradshaw to shame. He often picked up an extra shirt or sweater for Mark when he was making the rounds of his favorite designer boutiques. Mark himself favored Brooks Brothers and Patagonia, but his dad preferred to buy him the more expensive brands that he liked. After the arrest, I came across Mark cleaning out a hall closet in our Greenwich house.

"What are you doing?" I asked, pulling a suede jacket I loved out of the garbage bag he was filling with clothes. "This is what you wore on our second date!"

"My father gave it to me," he answered grimly, stuffing it back in the bag.

His alienation from Ruth had not yet reached that stage, but it was headed that way. Following the advice of his lawyers and his own heart, Mark was still maintaining a cool distance from his mother, who had lived with Bernie until the day he was sent away to prison, and continued afterward to accept his collect calls and visit him. His curt but sympathetic e-mail to her on the day she was evicted from her home by U.S. marshals hadn't, to Ruth's disappointment, led to a reunion with her eldest son.

I was the one who had softened and stepped into the role of peacemaker. It made me feel helpful. I wasn't covered in muck the way the rest of the Madoffs were, either. And truth be told, I gobbled up Ruth's gratitude, feeling acknowledged at last after years of being reminded that I was Mark's second wife. But I had a newborn and a two-year-old to care for, too, and the neediness of my husband and my mother-in-law was more than I could handle. They both left me drained. A final summer in Nantucket would give me a break from trying to fix everything for everyone else. I just wanted us to escape, to float away for a brief while in our own fragile little bubble. Most of all, I wanted my husband back, the old Mark. Maybe the change of scenery would give him fresh perspective and show him that we could make it back to shore if only he could stop thrashing against the current that was so much stronger and swifter than we were.

My determination was fueled by a deep faith in our justice system. There are days now when I beat myself up for believing this so fervently back then, but I was convinced that the truth would always win out. My stepdad was my living proof of that. Growing up, I had heard about Marty's famous First Amendment cases at the dinner table and sometimes watched him in the courtroom. When I was twelve, he had commanded national headlines in a libel case against CBS and Walter Jacobson, a wildly popular Chicago news anchor who had falsely accused a tobacco firm of secretly strategizing to seduce minors into taking up smoking. The tobacco firm had not only rejected the proposed marketing campaign aimed at "starters," but also fired the advertising agency that proposed it. My mother took my brother and me out of school for a special trip to Chicago to watch Marty present his closing argument. We were thrilled when he pointed to us and used our names in an analogy about stolen cookies from a cookie jar and the telltale evidence of crumbs on our mouths. Marty won a landmark $3 million verdict for his client. We won, too: for months afterward, Marty's fans sent chocolate chip cookies to Rob and me. I was so proud that I was Marty's stepdaughter, and even at that tender age, the righteousness of what he told the court resonated: It didn't matter what you thought of tobacco companies, or what presumptions or misgivings you harbored about the way they do business; at the end of the day, all that mattered was the truth. Everything else was just noise.

Mark needed to learn how to turn off the noise. But he loved technology and gadgets, and he couldn't stay away from the Internet, no matter how much we all pleaded. "Don't cruise the Web, don't read the *New York Post* and trash papers, and don't watch junk TV like CNBC, which is just full of publicity seekers like Donald Trump," Marty admonished. Trump was before the TV cameras within days of Bernie's arrest to assert that "of course the brothers were guilty." He wasn't the only publicity hound milking the scandal, to be sure, but he was one of the most reckless.

"Stop listening to it all. It doesn't mean anything," Marty told Mark again and again. Each time a new article or item appeared, Mark freaked out. Marty would patiently go over it with him, interpreting the journalese, pointing out that unnamed sources, rank speculation, and mere regurgitation of what was already out there did not add up to anything new. And if there was genuine cause for concern, Marty explained, Mark's lawyers would catch wind of it before some basement blogger or Donald Trump did. Mark would be temporarily reassured, but then he would head straight back to the computer, and the cycle of disbelief and despair would start all over again. It was a compulsion he couldn't seem to control.

Mark spent most of his waking hours reading everything he could about the case and its developments. News reports, gossip, blogosphere blather, even the jumbled comments from anonymous cranks, conspiracy nuts, and lonely lunatics. Mark was his own aggregator, and he had no filters or firewalls. Once we arrived in Nantucket, I thought that if anything, the beach would pry him loose. Mark had always been athletic and outdoorsy, and water was his element. When my first attempt to coax him into letting go flopped—he claimed his bum shoulder hurt too much to try surfing—I went on to Plan B.

"Let's do the New York City Marathon together!" I proposed. I had always wanted to run the famous 26.2-mile race, which was four months away, in early November. "C'mon, we can spend the summer training together. It'll be so cool." We were both runners, and I thought tackling the world's biggest road race would bring us back together as a couple. Having something that exciting to focus on would be good for us, and the endorphins sure couldn't hurt, either. It seemed like the perfect antidote for six months' worth of pent-up stress.

"Running hurts my knees," Mark protested. "But you should go for it, Steph." My disappointment was tempered by his eagerness to help me train, and I decided to enter the race without him. I was flabbergasted to learn that I would have to get permission from the lawyers first, since securing a number would require that I raise money. The marathon attracts more than a hundred thousand applicants a year, and all the individual spots were already taken. If I wanted to compete, I would need to sign on with a charity's team. I chose Lance Armstrong's Livestrong. To clinch a charity spot, though, you had to solicit donations and raise a certain amount of money for your entry fee. It was just a few thousand dollars, but our legal team nixed it.

Optics again: The press would have a field day writing about a Madoff family member asking people for money.

I ended up just paying the donation out of my own pocket, and started training on the treadmill Mark moved out onto our covered porch for me. Our house occupied a prime stretch of beachfront property, and the ocean view was magnificent. While Nicholas took his morning nap and Mark played with Audrey down on the beach, I would put on my iPod and listen to a playlist of upbeat songs, slipping into the zone while watching the waves curl to frothy peaks and then crash to shore. I started out at six miles, then eight, then ten, until I finally got up to thirteen. I felt ready to get off the treadmill and tackle a long run. Mark set out to chart a twenty-mile route for me around the island. On the big day, I left at seven a.m. to beat the heat, and ran to Milestone Road, the main drag heading toward the center of the island. I turned and pointed myself toward the red-and-white-striped Sankaty Lighthouse and called Mark when I hit the halfway point of my course. He drove out to meet me with water. I was feeling really good. *This isn't so bad,* I thought.

Two miles later, I changed my mind. I could see the famous lighthouse in the distance, but it didn't seem to be getting any closer. It was getting hot out. My feet were aching, and my legs were growing leaden. I finally made it to the lighthouse and snapped a picture with my phone as I trudged past. I still had miles to go. I stopped at Sconset Market and downed a Gatorade. I was so drenched in perspiration, my sneakers were squishing. I made my way back to Milestone Road only to have the sun burning in my face the rest of the way. By the time I got back to the house, I was in serious pain. My hips felt as if they would snap. Mark, Audrey, Nicholas, and our babysitter, Petal, were waiting at the end of the driveway for me, clapping. Mark was incredibly impressed. "Wow," he congratulated me. "You should be so proud of yourself." I limped straight to the shower and let the hot, hot water soothe my screaming muscles.

There were some hopeful signs that Mark was starting to come around as the summer yawned lazily before us. I was ridiculously happy when he picked up a fishing pole again for the first time. "You should take the boat out," I prodded him. Mark had a little black Boston Whaler he kept in Nantucket, but now he refused to remove the fishing boat from dry dock, fearing that someone might snap a picture of him and sell it to the tabloids, or that the Nantucket regulars who recognized him would pass judgment. The boat was named *Little Bull*, after the $7 million superyacht named *Bull* that Bernie had bought in 2007 and docked off the French Riviera near his Cap d'Antibes apartment. The yacht was an extravagance topped only by the private jet Bernie bought the following year. Professional decorators had outfitted both, sparing no cost. That Mark was afraid of anyone equating his Boston Whaler with his father's ostentatious lifestyle was maddening.

"You're crazy, just enjoy it!" I urged Mark. I hated the way he punished himself for what his father had done, caving in so readily to the popular sentiment that if you were a Madoff, you had no right to relax, or have fun, or feel anything but shame and remorse.

"If I want to go fishing, I'll just go with my friend Mike," Mark replied.

Every morning, he would drive down to the gas station/tackle shop and buy a bucketful of live eels to use as bait for the day. Standing on the beach in his cargo shorts and T-shirt, he would cast for sharks, striped bass, and bluefish. He would proudly grill his catch, eating even the bluefish, which I found disgusting. He became something of a local attraction for other beachgoers when he would reel in the four-to-five-foot young brown sharks, or duskies. People would come running to snap pictures before he threw them back, still thrashing. Even he had to laugh: Now we had beach paparazzi. None of them had any idea who Mark was. Once they'd seen his catch, though, the summer renters would never go back in the water.

As much as he loved New York, Mark just seemed to fare better out of the city after his father became Villain of the Year. I had noticed it early on, when I forced him to go with me to New Jersey to see a *Dancing with the Stars* stage show. Mark was a devoted lover of serious theater who had been courted to be on the boards of the Lincoln Center and Public theaters; I was an unabashed fan of anything campy. We had come to a reasonable compromise: I would suffer through his six-hour Shakespeare productions if he would go to Cher and Madonna concerts with me. (He drew the line at Justin Timberlake.) When the *Dancing with the Stars* tour came our way a few weeks after Bernie's arrest, I ordered tickets for the nearest venue—an arena in Newark—and made plans for a big date night. It was hysterical. I thought it was the coolest thing ever. We got lost driving through the wilds of New Jersey and spent most of the evening just laughing. It was sweet and delicious, like gulping fresh air into your lungs after escaping a big wildfire. Mark swore me to secrecy: "You can never tell anyone I agreed to go to that." We laughed even harder.

Nantucket wasn't a complete escape from notoriety, though. One morning after we first arrived, I woke up and headed out for a run. In the neighborhood, it's local custom for people to paint their family name on a large boulder at the foot of their gravel driveways. At the end of our driveway that day, I noticed that someone had vandalized our boulder with a pen, so it now read *Made off w/ everyone's $*. I was pissed and I was scared, remembering the death threats around Christmastime. I decided to paint it over with a meaningful message of my own.

"Wait! Don't look, don't look yet!" I called to Mark as I got to work. I knew he was worried that I was painting FUCK YOU in big block letters—a message he himself seriously contemplated having tattooed across his back. I've always been big on showy threats but weak on follow-through. Mark hovered warily. Finally I was done, and revealed my masterpiece: I had painted the boulder white and then used black paint to re-create the tattoo I had recently gotten on my forearm. It was the Chinese symbol for courage, copied off a leather-strapped bracelet Mark had given me that spring. Mark agreed that my Courage boulder was cool. I made the mistake of sending a photo to my stepdad.

"Get rid of that rock! What are you doing?" Marty shot back. He was worried that I was just going to draw more attention to the house, and I realized he had a point. But it had felt good, for that one afternoon, to push back against the nameless, faceless haters.

Out on my surfboard, no one knew or cared who I was. There was a fun camaraderie among surfers, and I reveled in the anonymity as I bantered with the college kids recounting their drinking escapades the night before. I would wait for a wave to surge beneath me, to feel the way it tugged backward ever so slightly, my signal to scramble to my feet, the nearby instructors shouting encouragement: "Pop up, pop up, pop up!" Getting up was always harder than staying up, but once I was standing, the wave was mine. Giddy and proud, I would ride it to shore, where my husband hung back, applauding my bravado.

It seemed like we were always in different places that summer, drifting apart then briefly coming back together, only to drift again. The tension would sometimes whip between us like a live wire. I was still intent on moving, and loved to browse real-estate sites and tour houses for sale online, imagining us snug and happy in the professionally staged family room photos, playing with the dog and grilling burgers in the pretty backyards, tucking the kids in at night in bedrooms where other children had wished the moon good night and then grown up. Our Mercer Street apartment had too many soured memories now.

"I'm sick of this. I can't live like this anymore," I screamed at Mark during one fight there. "I've got to get out of here. I'm over it!"

I thought my suggestion of moving to Greenwich would please him, and I had dragged him out one weekend when we were there to just drive by a house near the one we owned. I wanted to sell the old house for someplace that would belong to the new Mark and Stephanie, with no family history or Madoff ghosts attached. I was trying to show Mark that I wanted a life, and I wanted a life with him. I prattled on about how we would save money by not having to put our kids in private school, and how we would move back to the city once they were in college. I wasn't just looking to the immediate future; I was fast-forwarding eighteen years.

Mark angrily accused me of being passive-aggressive. I was getting tired of walking on eggshells with him. I never blamed him for the mess we were in, but it still pained him to see me get upset about it, and I could never bring up anything about the case. If he introduced the topic, I could respond, but I had to read his mood carefully and know when to retreat. When I could no longer bottle in my frustration or anger, and blew, Mark would react defensively.

"Well, how do you think I feel?" he would snarl. "I've lost my parents. I've lost my life. I've lost my job and I'll never get another one. You think you've got it bad?" He understood that I, too, had a right to be upset, but he always insisted that he had a right to be more upset. That was the saddest part to me, that we had somehow become two separate refugees in this disaster zone. Even in our worst moments, though, I didn't want to leave Mark. I wanted to find him, reclaim him, and restore us. What we had in each other was too valuable to forfeit.

I know Mark was frightened, because he was seeing an assertive,

fiercer side of me he had never seen until that summer. I was beginning to stand up for myself and express my frustrations and anger
more clearly, instead of just whining or complaining. Both Mark and
I had been seeing therapists for several months by then, and I could
feel myself shedding the put-up-with-it-and-shut-up girlfriend per-
sona I had been stuck in for so long. Mark's therapist was more of a
life coach, and Mark used his sessions to strategize about finding a new
career for himself. In my therapist's office, the focus at first was all
about Bernie. I wanted to know what made him tick, and how he had
fooled us all for so long. Was he mentally ill? A narcissist? A socio-
path? My therapist finally theorized that he showed signs of vertical
split personality, meaning he could essentially live a double life, dis-
avowing the repugnant one in much the same way as a sexual pervert
or binge eater might. I realized that I had some unfinished business
with Bernie.

"I'm going to write him a letter," I told Mark as we unpacked
groceries one day in our Nantucket kitchen. I was deeply, morbidly,
curious about jail, and wanted to know Bernie was suffering. I wanted
details. I wanted to know how cold and uncomfortable the cot was
after a lifetime of 800-thread-count Egyptian cotton linens and Euro-
pean goosedown comforters. I wondered what he woke up thinking.
I wanted to hear how isolated and lonely he felt, how bored he was,
how grim the rest of his life would be. And most of all, I wanted to
make Bernie Madoff suffer some more.

"If you do this, this is your decision. I don't want anything to do with it," Mark said. Glued to his computer again, he had come across a jailhouse interview Bernie had given some lawyers recently. "I don't give a shit about my sons," they had quoted him as saying.

While the kids were napping one sunny afternoon, I went up to my room, closed the door, and took out a notepad. I wanted us to be in Bernie's mind, in full Technicolor, because I thought it would be painful to sit in his jail cell and think about the life he had thrown away, to hear about everything he was missing out on. I carefully crafted a letter full of news about the beautiful summer we were having in Nantucket, describing Mark fishing on the beach and Audrey building her sand castles. I noted how fast the grandson he had never met—and never would—was growing. I tucked it in an envelope along with a drawing of a spider that Audrey had done, thinking the picture would tug at his heartstrings. I mailed it off, feeling gratifyingly vindictive.

Within a few days, a three-page reply came back in Bernie's loopy backhand. He was delighted to hear from me. He compared prison to a college campus, with "lovely lawns and trees." He lived in a dorm with twenty-four other inmates who all treated him with respect and admiration, calling him "Uncle Bernie" or "Mr. Madoff."

"I am quite the celebrity and treated like a Mafia Don," he boasted. He had "loads of friends," and the staff was sweet and considerate. There was never any violence or fighting, and prison was actually "much safer than walking the streets of New York." He was pumping iron, and had plenty of recreational classes and activities to choose from. Ruth had come for a four-hour visit, and they spoke by phone daily.

My plan had backfired.

Over the next eighteen months, though, I was oddly compelled to sporadically keep up this bizarre correspondence. I had become trapped in my own mind game. Even if Bernie couldn't see through me, I enjoyed my own cruelty. When a self-proclaimed mistress of Bernie's published a tell-all memoir, I taunted him about it. He denied the affair, describing the supposed paramour as a business acquaintance who had propositioned him and turned stalker after he shunned her advances. "Ruth believes me," Bernie asserted. That much I could easily accept as the truth: Bernie Madoff had swindled thousands of people out of billions of dollars, but surely Ruth had been his biggest sucker of all. The others made the mistake of giving him their money; she had given him her life.

The purported affair was one of the few Bernie-related topics Mark and I could safely discuss over a glass of wine without Mark getting upset or shutting down. When the book had surfaced, we followed the gossip and ultimately concluded it was a hoax. For one thing, we couldn't see when Bernie would have had any window of opportunity to cheat, if he had been so inclined. He and Ruth had always been joined at the hip, save for a single trip Ruth took to South Africa to go on safari with friends. Bernie had refused to go, saying it was because he wouldn't be able to get reliable cell phone reception there. He preferred vacations on the French Riviera. For a man with gorgeous yachts, a private jet, and unlimited funds, Bernie had very little curiosity about the world. His lack of culture was rather startling. He could be sitting in a Michelin-starred restaurant featuring the finest cuisine, and Ruth would be anxiously scanning the menu for him, fretting loudly, "What can Bernie eat, is there anything Bernie will eat?" World-class kitchens would have to whip up a pizza margherita, pasta with a simple meat sauce, or a steak without a potato. (Ruth's disapproval of carbs often extended to the ones on Bernie's plate.) Prison fare no doubt suited him perfectly.

That August, Bernie's chief lieutenant and longtime protégé, Frank DiPascali, pleaded guilty to ten criminal counts in connection with the Ponzi scheme. He was looking at 125 years in prison. The news unleashed fresh media speculation about indictments and arrests yet to come; as usual, Mark and Andy were dragged through the mud, even though both had cooperated fully with the investigation and nothing linked them to their father's criminal enterprise. Mark went into another tailspin and called my stepdad in a panic. Every time the feds arrested an accomplice of Bernie's, there was a chance he or she would attempt to barter for a reduced sentence by falsely implicating Mark and Andy. Intellectually, Mark understood Marty's repeated assurances that it takes more than a pointed finger to lock a cell door. There had to be corroborative evidence, which there wasn't, so Mark should stop worrying. Besides, all the people arrested were seventeenth-floor employees who had never worked with Mark (he and Andy ran their business from the nineteenth floor). That said, the anti-Madoff hysteria was tremendous, and public pressure on the authorities investigating the fraud had to be intense. The fear of being unjustly accused was always in Mark's gut. It tortured him.

Frank DiPascali was the prize catch in the government's net that summer, and reports that he was cooperating with investigators—unlike Bernie, who had clammed up after confessing—fueled the media speculation that he had something big to offer. Bernie and his accomplices had spent years masterfully deceiving rational, intelligent people. They were convincing liars. What if one of them decided to concoct damning stories about Mark in exchange for leniency? The speculation and Mark's paranoid nightmare both proved for naught: There was never any indication that DiPascali had anything bad to say about Mark or his brother.

Mark, Andy, and their uncle Peter were all named in a suit the court-appointed trustee had filed, alleging they should have detected the fraud and accusing them of living large off the fortune Bernie stole.

By the time we were packing up to leave Nantucket and head home to Mercer Street at the end of August, Mark's mood had shifted yet again. He had been contemplating ways to get back to work all summer, and he had hatched a plan he was eager to put into action: He was going to put his Internet obsession to good use and compile a daily insider newsletter about the real-estate industry. He had discussed the proposal with friends and potential clients, and felt confident that it would be well received. He would be able to put his expertise to use and bring in a small income. I was excited about my career, too: I had been accepted to graduate school and was taking two courses in the Child Life program at Bank Street College of Education starting in the fall. We arrived back in Manhattan with high hopes. We had barely unpacked before the mudslide hit us full force again.

Mark and I went out one afternoon to take Nicholas and Grouper for a walk. Mark was pushing Nick in his stroller when a strange woman rushed him with a video camera pointed in his face.

"Mr. Madoff! Mr. Madoff!" she screeched. "Are you scared you're going to lose your home?"

I spun around and covered her camera lens with my right hand and shoved her away with my left. She backed into a brick wall and started screaming at me. "Ma'am, this is my personal property! You have no right to touch my personal property!" Mark was already running away, crossing Broadway, and leaving me behind with the baby and the dog. I hurried back up the street, my hand throbbing, my temper smoking. I left the baby and Grouper with our doorman and tore back out again. I was going to go after that hideous bitch. I would hunt her down. Maybe all those boxing lessons I took to lose my baby weight hadn't been such a good idea after all, because I was ready to start swinging. As soon as I got outside, I spotted the camerawoman across the street, thanking the attendant in the garage where we parked our car. She obviously had paid him to tip her off about when we returned from Nantucket. I marched up and got right in her face.

"What a pathetic job you have, chasing after a family walking a baby! Is this what you like to do? Do you enjoy this? Do you find satisfaction from this job?"

She blanched, then threatened to sue me.

"Yeah, well, get in line," I replied before turning away, knowing that if I stayed, I just might punch her. Her freelance footage of me pushing the camera away later turned up on CBS.

Back home, Mark was waiting, chagrined.

"Why'd you leave me there?" I demanded.

"Because they want me, not you," he said. He thought she would chase after him if he ran; he hadn't counted on me going all Rambo.

That fall, our marriage was also engulfed by the scandal. Mark and his legal team wanted me to hire a matrimonial attorney to protect my marital assets when scores of devastated victims who were wiped out by Bernie began filing civil suits to try to recover some of their losses, often naming Mark and Andy as defendants along with their disgraced father. I asked a friend for a referral, and she sent me to Nancy Chemtob, a stylish and wickedly funny blonde who was considered tops in her field. Mark was standing in the kitchen when I placed the call late one afternoon. The watchdog receptionist didn't put me through, of course, but took my name. Fifteen seconds later, Nancy rang back. Mark and I both laughed at how quickly the Madoff name made lawyers jump these days. We met a couple of days later.

"Stephanie," she began with typical bluntness, "what percent of you wants to get a divorce?" I didn't hesitate.

"Zero percent." I just needed Nancy to help me hold on to what was rightfully mine. But the presence of a divorce lawyer for any reason spells trouble, and while it may have been the right legal strategy, it was painful for Mark and me. Nancy met with Mark as well, and twice she told him that I had no desire or plans to divorce him.

"You hired a divorce lawyer!" he would rail.

"Because *your* lawyers told me to!" I reminded him.

"Yeah, but you had to go out and hire the most aggressive divorce lawyer in New York!" he said with a smile. Even he had been charmed by Nancy.

We settled uneasily into our new routine, trying to move on. I was excited about my classes, and Mark dove into his newsletter with a sense of purpose and enthusiasm, getting up at four each morning to start gathering industry news. It was a good way to get his foot back into the working world, without having to face his paralyzing fear of searching for an actual job. Mark had once sold sneakers at FootLocker in high school, but had gone from college to working for his dad, and didn't have any experience at job hunting. He had never had to put together a résumé, network, make humbling cold calls, or sit across from an interviewer.

In late September, *60 Minutes* ran an interview with Irving Picard, the trustee in charge of liquidating Bernie's assets for his victims, and David Sheehan, Picard's chief counsel. I sat in front of the TV in our living room to watch; Mark stood at the kitchen counter, nursing a Scotch, listening as correspondent Morley Safer interviewed the pair. Eighteen billion dollars, Sheehan said, was still "just missing."

"Of all the people that should have known, his brother and his sons who worked under the same roof with him should have known," Safer declared.

"One would think so," Picard agreed.

Sheehan said that he thought "clearly they would have to have known what was going on." Safer didn't ask if there was any evidence that Mark and Andy knew of, or had participated in, any wrongdoing, and Picard offered none, but indicated that this wouldn't stop him from driving the Madoff brothers into the ground. Left out entirely was the fact that the market-making division run by Mark, deemed to be operating legally, had been successfully sold to another company for many millions of dollars.

"Whether or not they have a criminal problem, we will pursue them as far as we can pursue them," Picard said, "and if that leads to bankrupting them, then that's what will happen."

When the segment ended, I turned to Mark, feeling ill.

"These men scare me," I told him. He was furiously chewing his bottom lip and didn't even acknowledge me. Once again, this was only happening to him, not to me, not to us. I never doubted for a minute that Mark would be able to get us on solid footing again and rebuild a career that would provide a comfortable life for our family. My anxiety came from never knowing when the next bomb was going to drop. Mark, on the other hand, was convinced that each one would destroy him.

"I'm going to give Marty a call," he said, picking up the phone and turning to my stepdad for advice and consolation. There would be a conference call with the legal team and Andy first thing in the morning. Mark was still livid when we went to bed. He flicked on his Kindle and buried himself in one of the political thrillers he read for escape.

Our legal team issued a statement calling the allegations "entirely baseless."

Mark and Andrew Madoff had no prior knowledge of Bernard Madoff's crimes and contacted the U.S. Department of Justice and the SEC immediately after their father told them he had defrauded his investment advisory clients . . . Mark and Andrew Madoff were not officers of Bernard L. Madoff Investment Securities, LLC. They were employees with no ownership interest in and no access to overall financial information about BLMIS. They ran an operation that executed approximately 60 million trades per year for U.S. brokers, and their compensation was tied to the legitimate proprietary trading and market-making businesses they spent 20 years building. As they have from the beginning, Mark and Andrew continue to cooperate fully with the authorities in their ongoing investigations.

Nineteen days later, Mark tried to kill himself.

It was a beautiful Wednesday in October, and my mom and I had gone with Audrey on a preschool class trip to pick apples in the morning. We had plans to see a matinee of *The Lion King*. Mark had meetings with some people about the newsletter and came home around five. We fed the kids and gave them their baths, and I went to check my e-mail. There was one from Ruth, breezily telling me that she had just had *the most wonderful time with Kate and Daniel up at Susan's*. All these months, I had been there for Ruth, and I was the one who had gotten Kate and Daniel back into her life after Bernie's arrest, arranging visits with them for her at our home in Greenwich. I was under the impression Susan wasn't speaking to Ruth. In an instant, that old rivalry flared again, and I lost it.

"I can't deal with your mother anymore," I snapped at Mark. "She plays both sides of the coin. You know what? I can't stand it. I'm writing her a nasty e-mail back!"

"Don't," Mark pleaded. I ignored him and went to my computer. *Glad you had a nice dinner with Susan and thanks for the dagger,* I wrote Ruth. I went back at it with Mark.

"I don't understand why that controlling bitch is always in our life," I said of his ex. "Mark, you know how helpful I've been to your mother! I found a shrink for her! I helped her look for apartments. My friend offered her free PR advice. I've let her see the kids, and had her over for dinner."

The fight escalated until Mark left a little before nine.

"I'm going out for a walk," he said. He didn't take Grouper. He'd done this before to avoid fighting, and always came back after five minutes. This time he didn't. An hour passed. I called a girlfriend to vent and hung up after half an hour. Mark still wasn't home. I tried to call him and heard his phone ring. Mark never left without his iPhone, never once forgot it. I knew he had intentionally left it behind. I found it in the kitchen, picked it up, and smashed the screen against the corner of the granite countertop. I called my friend again.

"He's not coming back," I told her. This was the first time in our entire relationship that I couldn't reach him. My frustration soon turned to panic. I called my parents, who tried to calm me down. I dialed a few of Mark's friends, playing calm, asking each one, "Is

Mark with you by any chance?" It was close to midnight. I knew if I called the police, it would be a story in the paper, but I didn't care anymore. My instinct was screaming that something wasn't right. Fighting hysteria, I dialed 911.

"Hi. This is Stephanie Madoff. I'm really worried. My husband's been missing a few hours."

Two officers, a male and a female, showed up within ten minutes. I called my parents, and they rushed over, too.

"Please, please, you know who I'm married to, please don't tell the press," I begged the officers. "You know this name."

By the time my parents got downtown, half a dozen or more officers and detectives were in the apartment. I was still calling any friend of Mark's I could think of, but nobody had heard anything. The police had Marty call Ruth and told me to check with Susan, to see if either had heard from Mark.

"You think my husband's at his ex-wife's?" I asked incredulously. "I'm not calling that bitch." Marty did instead. One of the uniformed cops pulled Marty aside to ask whether Mark was expecting to be indicted the next morning. Then one of the detectives asked that we contact the building super to get access to the roof. My stomach lurched. I knew they were going up there to look for a body. They came back down, reporting there was no sign he had been up there.

"Was he on any medication?" a detective asked. He followed me into the bathroom, where I opened the medicine cabinet. Every pill bottle was missing. My knees buckled beneath me. "Oh, God," I sobbed. I had never been so scared.

Around five thirty a.m., the lead detective gently approached.

"Listen, we've got ten cop cars outside your building and about twenty cops inside the apartment, and you've got two young kids about to wake up. We don't want to cause a stir, so we're going to leave now. He'll show up."

I curled up in a chair, my parents waiting with me. Around eight, the babysitter let herself in.

"Petal, he hasn't come home," I cried. "I don't know what to do."

My mom put on a pot of coffee, and I went to take a shower. Over the sound of the rushing water, I thought I heard Mark say, "Hey," and saw a man walk past. I jumped out of the shower, grabbed a towel, and ran to the bed, where Mark lay on top of the covers, my stepdad hovering nearby. I flung myself onto Mark's chest, soaking wet.

"You're back, you're back," I wept, hugging him and kissing him again and again. I felt such relief, such happiness in that moment. I didn't notice at first how out of it he was. Marty called the police to let them know he was back, and two officers quickly arrived. One of them came into the bedroom with Marty while another hung back in the doorway.

"I still don't know how I got here," Mark said. His voice was too slow. "It was as if I walked here on autopilot. I took thirty Ambiens and did not expect to wake up. What the fuck does a guy have to do to kill himself?"

"Where were you?" Marty asked.

He said he had been at a nearby hotel. He had paid cash and registered under the name Mark David, dropping his last name.

"I wrote my father a note, took the pills, went to sleep."

"Where is the note?" Marty wanted to know.

"I dunno. Left it on the night table."

"What did it say?" Marty pressed him.

He recited his message: *Bernie: Now you know how you have destroyed the lives of your sons by your life of deceit. Fuck you.*

Marty called the hotel, intending to retrieve the note, but housekeeping told him the room had already been cleaned. He then dialed Adam, a friend Mark had been close to since childhood. An internist at NewYork-Presbyterian Hospital, Adam was stunned. He quickly arranged for an ambulance to pick up Mark. Marty called Andy to let him know, and Marty and I rode uptown with Mark, who was awake but groggy. In the emergency room, he was given apple juice and cookies and a purple paper gown to put on. He seemed terribly lost. He couldn't keep his eyes open or sit up. "I never want to see my mother again unless she stops talking to Bernie," he mumbled, drifting in and out of consciousness.

Andy showed up while Mark was being examined in the psychiatric emergency unit. Marty told him his brother had just tried to kill himself.

"Who says so?" Andy wanted to know.

"Your brother says so," Marty replied. Andy fell silent. He went in to see his brother and came back out, his face twisted in rage.

"Well, I've been given the wonderful job of telling my mother that Mark will never speak to her again!" he said. Mark had issued an ultimatum: Ruth had to choose. She would have to sever all ties with Bernie and publicly divorce him, or be cut off completely by us, losing not only her son but her grandchildren as well.

A psychiatrist emerged from the locked exam room where Mark was resting and recommended that I have him admitted to the hospital's psych facility in Westchester County, "because we would never be able to handle the press and the publicity down here." We weren't going to be able to go in the ambulance with him, so I came back downtown to pack some bags. I had decided that it would be better to make Greenwich our base of operations while Mark was hospitalized. It was quieter, and the commute was easier.

Marty and I dropped my mom and kids off at the house, then went together to see Mark. It was cold and rainy, and too dark too early. Winter was closing in. We walked down the empty hallways, looking for the Haven unit. It was the creepiest place I'd ever been in. The carpet was stained and dirty, and every wooden door we passed was closed tight. We finally found Mark's unit. There was a staffer posted outside his door to just sit and watch him for the first twenty-four hours. Protocol, we were told. I didn't know what I was supposed to do.

"You know, he swallowed a lot of pills," a nurse told me. It turned out to be many more than the thirty Ambien; he had gulped down Lorazepam as well, which he had been prescribed for anxiety. Just one could make you feel like you'd had several drinks. Thinking about him taking the pills freaked me out completely. I envisioned him swallowing them one by one, in a slow, determined assembly line, then imagined him swallowing them all at once in a desperate, horrible handful. Mark wasn't lucid enough to even know I was there.

The next day, he sent me a love letter from the psych ward.

Dear Stephanie,

Let me start by saying that you are the love of my life and always will be . . . When you look at me and smile, my world stops . . . I work so, so hard to prove to you how much you mean to me. I live my life for you. Even if it does not always feel that way, you need to know that everything I do is with you in mind. Without you, I'm empty. Not alone, empty . . . My mind is strong and I can always make it to the end if I know that you will be there waiting . . .

The night that I left, I was running because I had felt that I lost you and would never get you back . . . I was so frightened that so many other things had gotten in our way and that I could not get you to see me as the same person that you married . . .

Every day, I wake up and am haunted by the fact that my parents are gone. If they had died, it would have been better. If I had done something wrong, I would understand. But I did not. For my entire adult life, I have done the right thing. I have been respected by my colleagues, my family and my friends. Now, I am forced to carry the burden of the disgrace my father has caused. Nothing could be more selfish than to leave me with this legacy of shit. Somehow, I will dig my way out of this. But I need a lot of help.

You and I can't cure the world of bad people, so let's not try. It's too easy to let anger take over our lives. It's an awful feeling and it masks all that is good. You and I have endured more pain than any two people ever should have to. We can't let anger paralyze us.

I went to the grocery store and bought all his favorite foods: Twizzlers and sugared orange slices, chips and salsa, some energy bars, and all the ingredients for my lasagna, which he loved. We would have a hospital picnic. He would not remember any of it.

The doctors told us Mark should expect to be there a week to ten days. I found a notepad and pen and left bright little sticky notes in his room when he was gone for therapy. *I love you! I love you, we will get through this!* I signed them with hearts and smiley faces and X's and O's, as if I could transfer so much sunniness and optimism to him by osmosis.

The Haven was amazing. Any trace of creepiness quickly evaporated, and I was filled with gratitude for everyone who worked there. They were so compassionate, so gentle and skilled. Mark became himself again. I could tell that he valued and enjoyed what he had in life once more—he had focused so much on what had been taken from him that he couldn't see what he still had until now. This was our new beginning. He was deeply embarrassed by what he had done. "I know it was stupid," he admitted.

On the third day of his stay, Andy came to visit. I was sitting with Mark, and Andy shot me a look. Mark politely hinted that I should leave, walking me to the door. I excused myself reluctantly. It was pretty clear that Andy was there on a mission, and I had a bad feeling about it. He immediately lit into his brother.

"Fuck you! You're a stupid fucking asshole. How could you do this?"

They argued for about five minutes before Mark kicked him out. He had been looking forward to Andy's visit, and he hadn't been prepared for such an attack. After Andy left, Mark called me, crying hysterically. I had just pulled into the driveway of our Greenwich house. "You have to come back! Please come back! My brother just yelled at me. He was so mean to me." Marty went back to the hospital with me, and we found Mark lying in bed, still shell-shocked. I sat on the bed next to him and put my arm around him, rubbing his back.

"He called me a stupid fuck and told me he never wants to speak to me again," he recounted shakily. "Is that the way a guy talks to his brother who's in a hospital for trying to kill himself?"

By the time Andy heatedly confronted him in the hospital after the overdose, Mark was a scared, fragile shell of the strong, self-assured big brother Andy had always known. Their family was gone, destroyed by their father in a single blow. Despite his understandable resentment over being appointed Mark's messenger boy, Andy had dutifully relayed his brother's demand that their mother sever all ties with Bernie or be banished from our lives forever.

THE END OF NORMAL

Now I told Mark that his little brother was probably still just shaken by the suicide attempt. I told him not to listen, not to worry, that it would be okay. I'd been saying that for nearly a year, but the funny thing is, I never believed it more.

Andy was the only one Mark had left from the family I had thought was so solid, so loving and perfect. That Mark still loved his brother was painfully evident in the words he had groggily mumbled to my stepfather while we were waiting for the ambulance to take him to the hospital.

"I thought this would help Stephanie and my brother," he had said. Marty understood what he meant: Maybe this sacrificial condemnation of Bernie would move the government and its appointed trustee to finally recognize and acknowledge the Madoff sons' innocence. Maybe then, Mark's irrational and naïve reasoning went, they would leave Andy alone, and let me be, and we could move forward with our lives. Mark had been muzzled by his lawyers for a year, unable to tell his story and defend himself against people who presumed that the name Madoff made him a crook. If he couldn't say how persecuted he felt, he would show it.

I do know what I did was dumb, he e-mailed my stepfather from the psych ward. *But I just got overwhelmed . . . One of the things that got me that night was the constant attacks on who I am. Nothing is more important than my integrity, and for ten months, I have had to endure a public beating and I had no chance to respond. That's a brutal position to be in. I know that I must endure and I will. But it is so hard to be a public punching bag for so long and not fight back.*

The gravity of what had happened still didn't seem to register with Ruth.

Hi Stephanie, how are you? she breezily e-mailed me a few days later. *I've heard Mark is a little better. Can you let him know I love him and I've been thinking of nothing else . . . I know tomorrow is your anniversary and I didn't feel it was appropriate to send a card.*

Mark was discharged after a week. He seemed fresh, rested, and newly focused. He hadn't seen the kids yet. I had told Audrey her father was away on a fishing trip, and Mark and I stopped at a pet store on the way home to buy her a bright blue beta fish in a bowl. "Let's go home," I said.

Neither of us mentioned what had become obvious. Mark's mother had made her choice. His cry for help had been rebuffed by the one person he needed most in that lost, lonely moment when death seemed more inviting than life. Bernie could not be abandoned, but Mark could. What had been perplexing about Ruth's loyalty became, quite possibly, unforgivable.

seven

DECEMBER 2010

I was getting him back.

The months following Mark's suicide attempt were uneventful. I was afraid that being estranged now from his entire family would worsen Mark's despair, but he insisted that the intense therapy he had received at the Haven had given him a new perspective, and I noticed the change, too. I could actually see the old Mark beneath the sadness that had come to envelop him like a thin, brittle glaze. Even though the civil lawsuits had been piling up, he no longer seemed as obsessed as he had been with the smear campaign against him. Every free moment was no longer spent tethered to the computer, and I was relieved to see some sparkle again in his hazel eyes. Mark was finally beginning to believe he might be able to pull himself out of the mess his father left behind and rebuild a life for us.

Our good friend Joe hired him as an office manager in his high-end Wall Street head-hunting business just after his suicide attempt, and being back in the work world had given Mark a sense of purpose and identity again. The office was just around the corner from our apartment, and the casual atmosphere was the polar opposite of the stuffy formality that had defined Bernie's offices in the Lipstick Building. Mark banished most of his suits to a storage closet in the Greenwich house, saying they made his skin crawl now to even look at, much less wear. Joe kept his office in a hip loft with cool art on the walls and two boxer dogs, Winston and Lola, who served as receptionists. Mark usually took Grouper in to hang out, too. We rented a cottage in Montauk for the summer, and I felt like a newlywed again when I went to meet Mark's train from the city every Friday, anticipating our standing date for a romantic dinner before going home to the kids and spending the weekend playing with them on the beach.

That fall, we decorated the Greenwich house for Halloween, invited my family over, and took Nick and Audrey trick-or-treating. It felt like old times to hold hands on a chilly evening and laugh at how adorable our kids were as we went from door to door and then raided their treat bags as soon as they weren't looking.

A year into his new job, Mark had worked hard to prove himself, and it felt now more like a future than a favor. Mark was full of talk every evening about what had happened at the office that day. His real-estate newsletter was gaining momentum as well. I was taking my second year of child life classes in grad school and still volunteering at the hospital, which I loved, and it felt like Mark and I were getting ourselves on the same page emotionally again. He was allowing himself to feel a sense of optimism and even anticipation. We vowed to make the holidays enjoyable again, without the sense of dread that had hung over December for the past two years. Mark fired off e-mails to ten friends, inviting them over for drinks and hors d'oeuvres on Christmas Eve, and eagerly accepted the invitations that came our way. I allowed myself to hope that the fog of anger and self-pity that had engulfed him since he learned of his father's epic betrayal was beginning to lift at last.

Best of all that winter, we were starting to reconnect as a couple again. My heart soared like a lovesick schoolgirl's when Mark suggested we slip away after New Year's for a romantic three-day weekend in the Berkshires. We'd been hunkered down for so long, and he'd always panicked or lashed out at me when I'd suggested little getaways before. He had been too scared of bankruptcy to spend any money, and too paranoid about the media to risk being seen enjoying himself. Now we desperately needed some time to focus on our relationship instead of our situation. We had been married for only six years, and this mess already had consumed a full third of that scant time together. A short road trip to the picturesque mountains of western Massachusetts wasn't going to heal everything in our wounded marriage, but it was a promising start. I was more than willing to take that for now. We were in a good place.

Audrey had just turned four in November, and we had had a few friends and family members over for a cupcake and jewelry-making party, with the kids bashing away at a giant cupcake piñata hanging from an exposed steel beam in the foyer. Her big gift that year came from my parents: a trip to Disney World. My mother, Audrey, and I would spend four days there—the first time for all of us—and I knew we were in for a girly-girl extravaganza.

Audrey was beside herself with excitement at the prospect of meeting the Disney princesses in person, certain that they would recognize her as one of their own. She'd been wearing the costumes practically 24/7 for the past year. I'd always been something of a tomboy myself, and it cracked me up to see this miniature Cinderella in her shimmering blue ball gown, gliding across our living room floor on her scooter. I would wander into the kitchen in the morning to find Belle eating pancakes at the breakfast counter, with Grouper cast as the Beast, a role he was more than willing to take on when it involved table scraps falling into his vicinity. This was going to be the trip of her small lifetime, and I couldn't wait to see the expression on my daughter's face when she saw her fairy-tale idols for the first time. Mark was thrilled for her, too, and I felt a twinge of guilt about leaving him behind with the baby.

"Do you wanna come?" I offered.

"Naw, it should be an all-girls thing," he said. Nick was twenty-two months old, and already as rough-and-tumble as Audrey was dainty. Mark was looking forward to some serious male bonding, with juice-box binges and a *Night at the Museum* marathon. Nick so loved that movie that he had refused to leave when we'd taken the kids to the American Museum of Natural History the week before to pose for pictures in front of the giant Easter Island stone statue whose character in the movie says, "Hey, dum-dum! Give me gum-gum!" ("Where's the dum-dum statue?" Mark had asked the long-suffering museum guard who clearly answered that question all day long.)

Apart from spending some quality time with Nick, Mark had plenty of work to keep him occupied while Audrey and I were away. He and Joe were developing a business-oriented social media site, and Mark was still getting up at four every morning to put out the latest issue of his Sonar Report newsletter. Once that was done, he would enjoy his ritual alone time with a cup of coffee, then whip up some French toast or pancakes for the kids before strolling to work at 7:45. On the morning of December 8, Mark was busy making himself his favorite "turkey eggs"—scrambled egg whites with slices of turkey and ketchup or hot sauce mixed in—while I finished getting Audrey ready for our flight.

"Want a bite of turkey eggs?" he teased, knowing how revolted I was by his blue-plate special. He waved a forkful at me, laughing.

My mom arrived, along with our cab for the airport. I know Mark kissed me good-bye, but I can't remember that kiss anymore. I tell myself he didn't know then, that he hadn't decided yet that it would be our last.

"Sure you guys will be okay?" I fretted.

"Nick and I will be having wild parties," Mark assured me.

In the cab a few minutes later, I got my first text from him:

Hi, you know that you're going to JFK, right?

I smiled. This was the old Mark, my Mark. Before his father's disgrace had consumed him, Mark used to spend his entire day chatting with me via text or e-mail, our connection never broken. We would share pictures, links, one-liners, funny videos. We'd flirt, we'd fight, we'd gossip and banter, discuss and debate. Those thousands and thousands of little exchanges were the brushstrokes on a never-ending mural that was our story.

I texted him back from the plane before it pulled away from the gate.

We're on the plane. Is Nico up?

Then again once we arrived.

Just landed.

Cold or hot? Mark immediately wanted to know. The weather forecast had been unusually cold for Florida, and we'd been worried about rain. *How was Audrey? Nick slept til 7:30.*

I reminded him to e-mail Audrey's registration for summer camp, or the slots would fill up, and described the cheerleading team with crazy competitive mothers who'd been on our flight.

Audrey says she misses her daddy, I told him as we waited for the shuttle to the hotel.

That's good.

We headed for the park, where Audrey made a beeline for the nearest gift shop to replace her threadbare Cinderella gown with the latest in princess couture, which was, of course, the exact same dress. (Why do princesses only have one gown?) Properly attired, Audrey was ready to take in the Magic Kingdom.

It's a little overwhelming, I texted of our first impression at two thirty.

I know. Can be brutal. Do only what she can, Mark quickly advised. He'd done the Disney drill with Kate and Daniel when they were young. This was my first time. My mom and I may have been amateurs, but we were ready for the challenge: We had stocked the minifridge in our hotel room with a couple of bottles of wine before venturing out.

When Audrey caught sight of Cinderella's castle for the first time, my own eyes teared up at the look of pure wonder and joy on her little face. I was quick enough to capture the expression with my phone's camera and immediately sent the picture to Mark. Minutes later, I got a text message from him saying that the trustee was going to sue Audrey for $11,000 that Ruth and Bernie had gifted her.

Not a shock, Mark texted. *Still sucks.*

I was furious that he had just ruined such a happy moment for me, and sickened that the fallout from Bernie's crime was getting to the point of suing my four-year-old daughter in her Cinderella dress. For a sum that wouldn't even put her through preschool in New York, let alone turn her into some rich little heiress. It was pathetic. I punched back a response.

Why does shit like this always happen when I am finally trying to enjoy life again . . . Is it in the paper?

Mark assured me his lawyers were on it, and that there was nothing in the media. He tried gamely to placate me.

This stuff is nothing new, so enjoy Disney! That castle pic is adorable. Was she so psyched to see the castle?

He could just wait awhile, as far as I was concerned. I typed back a cryptic *Yeah* and ignored him for an hour while Audrey, delirious with delight, tried to take in her fairy tale come true.

Around five thirty, I tried to explain my anger and frustration to Mark. It was familiar ground by now, and even though I wanted him to keep me apprised of any developments that affected us as a family, I resented the timing of this bit of news. Couldn't I just go a few days without having to worry? Didn't Audrey deserve one hundred percent of me on this special occasion? Couldn't this once-in-a-lifetime memory be left untainted by Bernie?

I just hate that every f'g time I start to feel normal, something bad happens.

I understand. Mark sent me a peace offering: a photo of Nick taking his bath. I instantly melted, of course.

He is so cute.

The three of you keep me going, Mark answered. *Let's focus on that. You are all adorable.* He sent me a few more photos of the baby before signing off for the night. *Sweet dreams.*

Mark being able to let go of something Bernie-related and me fixating on it was a total role reversal for us. Maybe I had just been able to distance myself from it more in the beginning because I had been expecting Nick at the time and was determined to keep my stress levels in check and enjoy my pregnancy. But now little things were starting to get to me.

The latest arrest had just happened in mid-November, when Bernie's longtime associate JoAnn Crupi had been charged with helping perpetrate the Ponzi scheme. Jodi pleaded innocent, but faced up to sixty-five years in prison if convicted. I had met Jodi and her partner at one of the Madoff Montauk summer parties and had fallen in love with the two little boys they had adopted from Guatemala. Jodi and I had spent time sharing mommy stories, and she was the one who told me about the Elf on the Shelf tradition for Christmastime. After the scandal broke, though, my stepfather told me a very different story about Jodi.

In 2007, Marty had screwed up his courage and made an appointment to talk to Bernie in his office at the Lipstick Building about investing a million dollars of his retirement savings in the exclusive Madoff fund. Marty knew he was way out of his league—a piker by Bernie's standards—but he hoped the family connection would persuade Bernie.

"Marty, the truth is, the fund is closed and I am not taking any more investors," Bernie had told him. "But how could I say no to my *mispoche*? Sure, go see Jodi Crupi and she will give you instructions on where to send the money." Bernie stole Marty's money as readily as he stole everyone else's. Neither Bernie nor Ruth had attempted to contact my parents after Bernie was exposed. Jodi Crupi's arrest literally brought Bernie's crime home to me. The grand scope of what he had done was awful enough, but the true cruelty was in the casual intimacy of it. Bernie, by his own later admission to interviewers, had known by then that his scheme was unraveling. How could he have looked me in the eye for another year, sat at my dinner table, played with my daughter, knowing he had swindled my parents?

With the funk of Bernie and concern about the new lawsuit swirling in my head, I barely slept that night at Disney World. When I woke up, I could feel myself coming down with the cold that had already made its way through the rest of the family. Audrey finished her strawberry Mickey Mouse waffle for breakfast and I dragged myself out the door for another day in Fantasyland, hoping Audrey's excitement would energize me. We spent much of the morning standing in line so Audrey could have her picture taken with each and every princess, and Cinderella's wicked stepmother and evil stepsisters, too. "I'm a big fan of yours," I told the wicked stepmother, posing for a photo. "I'm a stepmom, too." I documented each VIP encounter and ride for Mark.

How's it going? Mark wondered at lunchtime. *The pictures are staggeringly cute. She looks like she's having the best time.* We caught up by phone that evening at the hotel, when Mark called as usual to say good night. All was well on the home front. My cold was getting worse, and after a full day in the park, Mom, Audrey, and I were ready to hit the sack early. We'd braved the total bedlam of the character dinner, with costumed characters visiting each table, and I was already dreading the character breakfast we'd signed up for on our last morning.

Nick has a little diaper rash.

That's sad. Are you having fun with him?

Oh yeah. Some wrestling this morning. Nick loved to roughhouse with his dad; I missed hearing his uncontrollable belly laughs as Mark tickled him.

We're waiting in line to meet Pluto.

He's my FAV!!!!!!!!!!!!!!!

Mark told me he'd gone to have the doctor check out some moles we'd been worried about; everything was okay, and he was just waiting on some blood work. Since his father's arrest, Mark had abandoned his gluten-free diet, and I was worried about his celiac disease. I'd been nagging him for months to have his liver enzyme levels checked and was glad he'd finally gone in. Mark had always taken good care of himself, and with two young children now, I wanted him to make that a priority again, to acknowledge to himself that he was worth it.

My cold is awful, I complained around three thirty. *Had to come back to room to rest.* My mom had taken Audrey to the hotel pool. We were planning on an early dinner at the California Grill. We were flying home the next afternoon. Mark messaged back his own plans for the evening: Petal was going to stay late and watch Nick while Mark went to our friend Trevor's holiday party. Friends were starting to RSVP for our Christmas Eve party, too, he reported.

Rest up for your nite. I miss u guys.

We kiss you too, I responded, quickly sending a correction. *I meant to say miss.*

Kiss is OK. Better than diss . . . I'm looking forward to getting our tree. Should be fun.

Just after six thirty, Mark forwarded a *Wall Street Journal* article that apparently ran online before it was to appear in the paper the following morning. MADOFF'S KIN EYED AS PROBE GRINDS ON, the headline read. "Federal prosecutors are ratcheting up pressure on one of Bernard L. Madoff's former 'back office' employees to cooperate with their investigation as they have continued in recent months to scruti-nize his brother and sons, according to people familiar with the situa-tion," the story began. The piece focused on Annette Bongiorno, who had been arrested a month earlier along with Jodi Crupi. The article made no specific allegations against Mark, Andy, or their uncle Peter, and included a statement from Mark's lawyer reiterating that Bernie's sons had no prior knowledge of their father's crimes, had turned him in as soon as he confessed, and continued to cooperate fully with authorities.

Mark was furious. *What the hell happened here? We did not know about this?* he e-mailed my stepfather.

Marty quickly dissected the piece and e-mailed his opinion. *A nothing new story with a manufactured bullshit headline. There is not a shred of news here. Nada. Pay it no mind, plse.*

Unappeased, Mark forwarded it to me. *This is an awful article. No idea that it was coming out. I'm beyond devastated . . .*

I missed the e-mail and, oblivious, replied an hour later to the text he had sent me about the Christmas tree: *I am psyched to get our tree, too. We are sitting with a view of Cinderella's castle. Audrey is freaking.* Soft lights gave the illusion that the castle was frosted with snow. The whole theme park was decorated to the hilt, making me nostalgic for the cozy holiday rituals we so loved, like the annual Christmas Stroll down Nantucket's main street, culminating with the arrival of Santa Claus on a Coast Guard cutter.

My reverie was broken fifteen minutes later, when I scrolled back through my e-mails and found Mark's rant about the *Wall Street Jour-*

nal piece. My heart felt like a stone in my chest. It wasn't the report itself that unhinged me—Marty was right, it was a thin rehash of old news—but Mark's response to it. It was like watching him disappear down the dark rabbit hole again. It scared me, and infuriated me. I was absolutely boiling with resentment: Couldn't Mark have waited for a day and let me enjoy this special time with Audrey and my mom without this toxic cloud reappearing over our heads? I sent him a frustrated reply.

Just saw the article and I CANNOT TAKE THIS ANYMORE!!!
U and ur legal team and ur PR team MUST do something!! I am so fucking pissed, so beyond mad. It's been 2 f'g years!! Enuf!

In an instant, we were right back in hell, where Bernie Madoff, sheltered and fawned over in his bucolic prison, rightfully belonged.

I'm doing my best to hold it together, Mark now texted me. *I need your help. I've called and shrieked at everyone, including Marty. I don't know what to do anymore. I've tried.*

My stepfather would later remember how enraged Mark was when he called that evening just as Marty was leaving his office. He had sat down on a sofa in the reception area near the elevators and spent twenty minutes listening to his son-in-law rant.

"Marty, how am I ever going to get a job after this?" he had demanded. The gig with his friend Joe was supposed to be a foot back in the business, not a long-term career. "Look at that headline! These people are destroying my reputation. I am ruined. Ruined. My reputation has been my lifeblood. I have spent my professional life building that reputation. Now they have destroyed it. How can they do that?"

Marty tried again to show Mark he was overreacting. The article was bullshit. There was not a hint of evidence that Mark had done anything wrong. "We know from experience that these pieces have a half-life of about twenty-four hours," he reminded Mark, "and this being a Saturday paper, even less than that. Three days from now, nobody will remember it." He knew that trying to totally resolve Mark's concerns was an exercise in futility when he got in this mode; his fear of being unjustly accused was, as Marty saw it, "baked in" by now. Fear, frustration, anger, and humiliation had formed a rock-hard core inside Mark that no amount of reason could penetrate. Marty knew he couldn't convince Mark, but he could calm him. That evening, hanging up the phone, he thought he had succeeded at that. They had ended their conversation the way they always did. They had become more like father and son than in-laws over the past two years.

"Thanks, Marty, what would I do without you? I love you," Mark said.

"I love you, too, darling," Marty replied. "Kiss the baby for me, and I'll see you soon."

I was too sick, tired, and angry to chip away at the rock anymore that evening. *I am turning my phone off,* I told Mark. He could reach me through the hotel switchboard if needed. *Enjoy Trevor's. Good night.*

Sent Petal home, he replied at 8:04 p.m. He was skipping the party. *Not up for it.*

At 4:14 on Saturday morning, December 11, 2010—the second anniversary of his father's arrest—Mark sent three short e-mails. I found two of them when I woke up and turned on my phone around 6:45. The first one said *Help* in the subject line.

Please send someone to take care of Nick

The next one, sent three seconds later, was blank, with these words in bold in the subject line.

I Love You.

Audrey was still asleep. My mom was up, making coffee. "Mom, I got these weird e-mails from Mark," I told her shakily as I dialed Mark's number. It went instantly to voice mail. I tried the house line. No answer.

"Mom, something's wrong." I fought the rising panic, willing myself to stay calm. Audrey was going to wake up any minute, and I couldn't let her sense my fear.

Mom looked at her e-mail and saw that she, Marty, and my brother, Rob, had been copied on the one asking for someone to come take care of Nick. She called Marty to send him to Mercer Street while I kept trying to reach Mark. I dialed the night doorman at our apartment building.

"Listen, I'm in Florida, and I just got two very upsetting e-mails from my husband. My son is in the apartment. Can you please check and see if everyone's okay?"

"Yes," he promised. "I'll go check."

I hung up and waited. Ten minutes passed. Audrey woke up. "Do you want another Mickey waffle?" I asked her, forcing a bright smile across my face, ordering myself not to cry. Fifteen minutes had passed. Why wasn't the doorman calling? I rang him again.

"Steve, did you go upstairs?" I asked.

"I needed to call the super," he said. "Mr. Madoff may not want me in the apartment that early."

I couldn't believe what I was hearing. "Please," I begged him. "Please. I'm scared. I am scared for my son."

He agreed, again, to go up to check.

Marty arrived just moments later, though, and went up himself. My mother's cell phone rang, and I heard her gasp. "Oh my God, oh my God." She turned to me, stricken. "He's dead, Stephanie. He's dead!"

"What?" I responded. "What? What do you *mean?*"

"Stephanie, he's dead." She tried to hug me. I pushed her away. I didn't even ask how he had done it. I wasn't ready to know that yet. My first vision was a bloody one of him on our couch with a knife, his throat slit open. There was blood everywhere.

In fact, my stepfather had found Mark's body hanging from an exposed steel beam that ran through the living room. He had fashioned a noose out of Grouper's leash. A snapped cord from the vacuum cleaner was on a table nearby; apparently it had taken two tries. Nick was sleeping in his nursery just a few steps away. Grouper had been shut in the room with him.

Marty rushed in to check on the baby while calling 911. A policewoman ended up giving my son his morning bottle. Rob arrived soon after the police and fell into Marty's arms as both men wept. Rob managed to get Nick dressed and put a baby blanket over his small head so he wouldn't see his father's body on the way out. Marty stayed behind to answer police questions, and watched his son-in-law's body taken away. Some fifty to one hundred reporters and photographers, alerted by the police scanners they monitor, were waiting outside when Marty finally came out with the dog and pushed his way through the throng, across our cordoned-off street, to the garage where his car was waiting. The photographers followed. Confused and frightened, Grouper struggled to back away from them and refused to jump in the car. "Can you please stop with the flashes until I get him into the car?" Marty implored. Even our dog was at their mercy now.

In Florida, I was dry-eyed and strangely efficient. I had to hold the shock at bay; there was no way I was going to tell Audrey such horrific news in a place that had been so magical to her. I called Bridget, our family babysitter in Greenwich, and told her what had happened. I asked her to pick up Nick at my brother's apartment and bring him to our Greenwich house, where I would meet them that afternoon. Bridget was close to Susan and had sat for Kate and Daniel when they were little, too. She would tell Mark's ex-wife what had happened. Marty told Andy, who in turn would tell Ruth. The prison warden could tell Bernie. Mark had not sent farewell messages to any of them.

My mother changed our flight. The next one was leaving for New York around twelve thirty. I had to get out of there immediately. All I wanted was to get home to my son. I packed our bags, tucking the Santa hat with Goofy ears that we'd bought for Mark in with the other cheap souvenirs he would never see. I called my therapist and asked what I should tell Audrey, sitting there happily in her Minnie Mouse costume, unaware that the father she worshipped had decided that she would somehow be better off without him. *I will never forgive you,*

Mark Madoff, I silently swore. The hotel staff lined up to wave good-bye to us.

"Have a magical day!" they chirped.

We were in the airport security line when I looked back at my mom behind us and mouthed the words: *How did he do it?*

She pantomimed a rope around her neck.

In the departure lounge, a text message popped up on my phone from a grad school classmate, telling me how sorry she was to hear the news. I was surprised—I used only my maiden name at school and had kept my personal travails of the past two years very private. News of my husband's suicide was on the TV mounted in front of us. I turned Audrey around on my lap and distracted her with a computer game on my iPad.

On the plane, I broke down completely, hiding my tears behind sunglasses, staring out the window. The sun was shining, the sky impossibly blue. *How the fuck am I going to get through this?* I wondered. *What am I going to do?* I was so very angry. I still am. If you let go of the rage, I knew even then, the sorrow moves in. As the plane descended into New York, clouds obliterated the last of the sun. The wintry landscape below was rendered in shades of black, white, and gray. The bleakness felt right to me. I still had to tell Audrey that she would never see her daddy again. I was filled with fear. I couldn't bear to face the press, face my friends, face living life alone.

I hate you, Mark Madoff.

When I turned my phone on, it was overflowing with messages and texts from friends who had heard the news. Andy called. "What do you want to do here?" he asked. We agreed that a funeral was out of the question. It would turn into a three-ring media circus.

"I'm so angry. I'm so angry right now, I just can't believe it," I told him. Andy was understanding and supportive. He was hurt and angry, too. For once, my brother-in-law and I were on the same page.

Audrey fell asleep on the drive to Greenwich. Pulling into our driveway, I was surprised that Bridget's car wasn't already there. I needed to see Nick the minute I got home. I called the babysitter's cell phone.

"Where are you?" I asked anxiously.

"Oh, we're about ten or fifteen minutes away," she told me. "He's sleeping in the car. He's fine." Only later would I discover she had taken him first to Susan's.

With Audrey still sleeping in the car, I went to open our front door and forgot to turn off the security system. The alarm started blaring; I was too flustered to get it to turn off. The Greenwich police arrived, and later sent me a bill for the false alarm. Audrey woke up, excited about seeing her daddy and brother again. She bolted for the house. I brought her upstairs to the master bedroom and sat down in an armchair. I had scripted the conversation in my head on the drive from the airport while she slept, remembering bits and pieces from the class I had just taken, called Loss in Children's Lives. I knew I had to be clear.

"I have to tell you something, and it's really sad. Daddy died."

"What? Am I ever going to see my daddy again?" Her huge brown eyes widened in hurt surprise.

"No. I'm so sorry, honey. You're never going to see your daddy again."

Audrey looked at me in disbelief.

"I want to see my daddy!" She began to cry. "I have to tell my friends. I have to tell Ella and Scarlett."

At that point, Bridget fortuitously arrived with Nick, and Audrey was distracted by the prospect of seeing her baby brother. I raced into the driveway, hugging him and hugging him as he slept in his car seat.

The afternoon passed in a blur of tears and phone calls. My two closest girlfriends, RoseMarie and Christi, came to stay with me. Marty handled everything with the coroner and the funeral home. People came by with food and flowers. Mark's lawyer, Martin Flumenbaum, arrived to offer his condolences. I learned that the third e-mail Mark had sent at 4:14 that morning was to him. The subject line read: *Stephanie*. Inside, two lines: *Nobody wants to believe the truth. Please take care of my family.*

"Enough! Enough! You get me out of this mess," I ordered Flumenbaum. "I can't take this anymore! This has to end! This has to end!" I would not let myself be swallowed by the same quicksand that had pulled and pulled at Mark until he no longer had the strength to fight it.

The lawyer told me the same thing he had told my husband countless times.

"I'll do what I can."

He released a statement to the media: *Mark Madoff took his own life today. This is a terrible and unnecessary tragedy. Mark was an inno-*

cent victim of his father's monstrous crime who succumbed to two years of
unrelenting pressure from false accusations and innuendo.

Night fell and I was a thirty-six-year-old widow with two small
children and a question mark where a life should have been. It was
after midnight when I went into the living room and grabbed every
vase, bowl, and porcelain knickknack I could hold. I went out the
front door and stood on the frozen lawn, hurling each and every fragile useless treasure to the ground until everything lay smashed and
shattered at my feet. I went back inside and found a favorite flannel
shirt of Mark's in the closet. I put it on and fell asleep in the scent
of him.

eight

No More Lies

Mark came to me in a dream that night of the eleventh, flickering in black and white like an old movie reel. He was in a T-shirt and gym shorts, just like he usually wore to bed, and he was holding a baby in his arms. He stood there in profile, and I couldn't see his face. Then, wordlessly, he was gone again. *Wait,* I wanted to call after him, *did you cradle your son in your arms before you decided to kill yourself outside his bedroom door? Did you kiss him good-bye?* My husband's visitation, like his death, left me sad and yearning for answers.

I woke up in Greenwich on December 12 wondering for a few seconds whether this was real, if it had really happened. I felt deserted in a combat zone. I couldn't believe he had done this to us. Audrey was still asleep in my bed, but I could hear Nick up and stirring. I didn't know how I was going to summon the energy to pretend for them that everything was going to be okay when I had no idea myself whether I would ever be whole again.

My stepfather was on the phone, making the necessary arrangements, and I felt a flood of love and gratitude. Marty was hurting, too, but he pushed his own pain aside to tend to mine. I couldn't imagine having a conversation with the medical examiner about my husband's autopsy or cremation. When he had arrived at the house with Grouper the evening of Mark's death, Marty had come into the kitchen and found me holding Audrey. "Hi, Grampa," she greeted him. "You know my daddy is dead and is never coming back again. He got sick in his brain, and when people get sick in their brain, they just die and don't come back. But he is in the sky, and I can talk to him all I want."

Cars full of reporters and photographers were already lining the narrow lane leading to our house, zoom lenses ready to catch an image of the grieving young widow. "Stay here, we'll go," Marty and RoseMarie insisted when I wanted to make my usual morning drive to Dunkin' Donuts for coffee. The two of them helped me craft a statement to the press, expressing my devastation and begging for the privacy to mourn. *My husband Mark took his own life and regardless of what you feel about my father-in-law and his monstrous crimes, Mark's children are innocent victims and this is tragic for them. I will miss him and love him forever.*

Over the next few days, friends trickled in to pay their condolences, and the house began to fill with food I couldn't eat and flowers I couldn't smell. The mail brought a jarring mix of sympathy cards and Christmas greetings. It was snowy and cold, and I remember looking out at the backyard and spotting the big gray crane we called Charlie. He was a summer bird and had never appeared in winter before. I wondered if he had missed his flock's migration south. I watched him swoop down from a bare tree branch, then circle the pond purposefully, as if in winged tribute. Some bewildered instinct was driving Grouper to brave the cold, too, and he sat expectantly in the driveway for hours that first week, waiting patiently for his master to come home.

Susan arrived that morning-after with Kate and Daniel, her husband, Rich, and their five-year-old daughter, Annabelle, as well as Andy's two daughters. Andy was conspicuously absent. "You saved him. You know you saved him," Susan said cryptically, enveloping me in a hug. I couldn't begin to fathom what she meant. How had I saved him? He was gone. I wrote the comment off to shock; she had been hysterical when told of her ex-husband's death. I steered her into the dining room for a private conversation. There was something I needed to say. Whatever distrust and ill will there had been between us all these years seemed pointless now.

"Susan, I need your help," I began. "Please, let's be on the same page. I don't want any more secrets. I don't want anything done behind my back. I can't take any more lies. No more lies." For two years, my life had been ripped apart by betrayal and dishonesty, and I was tired of being manipulated. I just wanted people to be straight with me, even if I wasn't going to like what they had to say. Susan seemed instantly receptive to my request.

"Of course, Stephanie," she assured me. "Rich and I are here for you, whatever you need." Her compassion gave me a surge of hope. If only we could have formed the same bond when Mark was alive! In that moment, I was deeply grateful for Susan's unexpected solidarity.

It didn't take long before I put my newfound friendship with her to the test. Feeling claustrophobic, I went with my mother to the village of Old Greenwich a couple of days later. A teenaged driver accidentally backed into my car, crumpling a rear door. My pent-up stress and anger exploded like a burst steam pipe, and I flew out of the passenger seat screaming at the poor terrified girl and her father. "Are you fucking *kidding* me?" I shrieked in the father's face. He called the police, and an officer showed up to take an incident report. My mother ordered me back into the car, where I sat fuming and cursing under my breath. I was suddenly desperate to just be home. My mom, who had been driving, was shaking, and I was too worked up to get behind the wheel myself. I called Susan to see if Daniel could come pick me up. "We'll be right there," she promised. She and Rich arrived within minutes. Seeing how rattled both my mother and I were, Rich chivalrously slid behind the wheel of the damaged SUV to take us home. "Oh my God," Susan said sympathetically, "this is the last thing you need."

Given the circumstances, I had decided that a very small, private memorial was best for saying our good-byes to Mark. Our dear friend Adam took on the tough task of letting friends and acquaintances know that there would be no funeral. Some were angry or disappointed that they weren't invited to attend, but most understood. RoseMarie was the one who got the call from Ruth Madoff. Ruth had sought—but not taken—RoseMarie's public relations advice about repairing her image in the media after Bernie's arrest. RoseMarie was struck by how flat and unemotional Ruth sounded now.

"I have to get into this memorial service," she told RoseMarie. "I have to get in there." She also wanted to speak to me directly. Like Mark, I had cut off contact after Ruth had refused his plea from the psych ward a year earlier to sever all ties with Bernie and publicly divorce him. Her decision had cut Mark to the core. She had chosen not to be in his life; showing up for his death struck me as unbelievably cold and selfish.

"No," I told RoseMarie. "Absolutely not. Mark would not want her there." Andy had recently begun acting as Ruth's conduit and, even though he was barely speaking to Mark himself, had relayed their mother's suggestion that the three of them get together when she visited Kate and Daniel over the upcoming holidays. Three days before he died, Mark had e-mailed her.

Mom. Unfortunately, I don't have it in me for the visit. I have so many unresolved things in my head that I can't begin to process them. I had hoped that my anger would subside, but it has not. In fact, all of the crap that is going on now has exacerbated the emotions. I know that you will be disappointed but I just can't do this now.

I assumed Ruth was calling RoseMarie from Florida, where she had been living off and on with her sister. As far as I was concerned, she could grieve with her own family; I wanted her nowhere near what remained of mine. My decision was as pragmatic as it was emotional.

Ruth was constantly stalked by the press, and it would have been like unleashing the hounds of hell to have her pull into my driveway. The post-arrest estrangement between the Madoff parents and their children had been widely reported, so a shot of Ruth coming to mourn her dead son would have no doubt fetched a handsome fee for the paparazzi lurking outside, while likely tipping off the media that a service was being held inside.

I just wanted this whole ordeal to be as quiet and private as possible, especially for the children's sake. Kate and Daniel were hurt and dazed, and Audrey was struggling to absorb her loss, too. I would find her skipping around the house in her polka-dotted Minnie Mouse costume from Disney World, singing out, "My daddy's dead and he's not coming back!" like some morbid nursery rhyme. I understood the impulse; I kept having to remind myself that Mark wasn't coming back, too. It was the mental equivalent of cutting yourself, the way angst-ridden teenaged girls sometimes do, to bleed a little over and over in hopes of slowly releasing the greater pain you know is building up inside. Saying Mark was dead, whether silently or out loud, was better than feeling it. When I looked at my own two precious babies, I couldn't imagine ever putting my needs ahead of theirs, of hurting them the way Ruth had hurt her son. RoseMarie bravely conveyed my sentiments to Ruth Madoff.

"Look, you were asked by Mark to stop all contact with Bernie over a year ago," she said. "You did not do that, and Stephanie feels strongly that because of that, you chose to stick by the man who not only ruined thousands of lives, but destroyed her life and that of her children, and killed her husband."

Ruth wasn't the only one I banished: The day of Mark's death, my brother, Rob, mentioned that Andy wanted to drop by. I hadn't eaten much that day, but had drunk a couple of glasses of wine that evening. "That's fine," I told Rob, full of liquid courage, "but I don't want that fucking bitch Catherine in my home, and neither would Mark."

My brother obediently repeated the gist of my drunken decree to Andy. "Well then, I'm not coming," he informed Rob. I, of course, had no memory of the whole incident come morning, and was perplexed when Mark's brother still hadn't paid his respects two days later. I was mortified when Rob recounted what I'd said. Marty played mediator and rang up Andy, who claimed paparazzi were swarming his apartment building in the city and he couldn't get out. "I'll try tomorrow," he promised. When he still didn't show, Marty called again, getting another excuse. Marty tried once more. "Marty, I cannot do it," Andy finally admitted.

"Look, Stephanie," my stepfather admonished me, "you should call him up and apologize." I still felt righteous, but I realized I wasn't the only family member reeling from Mark's suicide; I could only imagine how horrible Andy felt. The two brothers had been estranged for months after Andy erupted at Mark in the hospital following his first suicide attempt, and Mark had confided to me that their tentative steps toward reconciliation recently had felt strained and "just weird." Andy would suggest meeting in odd places, like at a bench in

Washington Square Park while he was on one of his long bike rides. Mark had killed himself before they could mend their relationship entirely. I dialed up Andy's girlfriend.

"I'm sorry I said that," I tearfully apologized. "You're welcome in my home. You know no one was happier than I was to see somebody make Andy so happy." That much was true. The fact that Andy was still married had pretty much precluded us becoming sisters-in-law, as much as I once would have dearly loved the camaraderie of another second wife in the Madoff clan. And even though my naïve BFF fantasies had been quickly dashed, Mark and I were both genuinely glad that Andy had found love. He was a quirky introvert who struggled socially compared with his sociable older brother. Mark and I had both wanted him to experience that joy of finding your true soul mate.

"Okay, Stephanie," Catherine responded now to my apology. "I'm sure Andrew will be a great help to you."

The service was scheduled for Thursday evening, five days after Mark's death. His ashes had come from the funeral home in a black matte metal box, and I was in no rush to decide what to do with them. During the day, I would set the box on a little end table in the living room, surrounded by our family photographs. At night, I would carry the ashes back upstairs when I went to bed, not wanting to leave him alone. I would place the box on Mark's nightstand.

This solitary ritual was a stark contrast to the external debate over what I should or should not do with my husband's remains. I was taken aback by the people who felt entitled, somehow, to a say. Bernie's younger brother, Peter, was hoping that Mark would be buried in the family vault he had bought in a Jewish cemetery following his own son's death. Mark had expressed outrage at his uncle back when Peter had informed us of his "gift." "You know my wife isn't Jewish!" Mark had objected, pointing out that I therefore could not be buried in a Jewish cemetery. Peter broached the possibility again after Mark died.

He wasn't the only one who had strong feelings on the matter. Even a former Madoff employee I barely knew felt the need to meddle in this most private of affairs. *I am begging you to please not cremate Mark*, he e-mailed me three days after Mark's suicide. *I have a grave plot in Staten Island which I would let him be in for free. I have connections and can make a couple of calls and have him taken and buried in a proper Jewish way, and hopefully no one has to know.* It would have all been so ludicrous if it hadn't been such a terrible shame. Mark probably would have been amused.

He had come to me again on my second night of being alone. I could feel him lying next to me in our bed, spooning me the way he always did before we drifted off to sleep together. It was wildly comforting, and for a moment, my fear and anger subsided. *He'll take care of me somehow*, I thought.

A couple of days before the memorial, I went upstairs to try to take a nap. I spent much of my time that week crying in my bedroom so Nick and Audrey wouldn't see me breaking down. As I lay there, though, it wasn't sorrow or exhaustion that overwhelmed me. It was rage. I shot out of bed, grabbed the phone, and tore downstairs. Marty and my brother caught a glimpse of me storming onto the back patio. I stood shivering in the cold and punched in a familiar number.

A leaden voice answered.

"Hi, Ruth, it's Stephanie." Stupidly polite.

"Hi, Stephanie." No emotion.

I lit into her with a fury so vicious and raw, I didn't even recognize my own voice.

"You stuck by the man who killed my husband!" I screamed. "What kind of mother *are* you? Why? Why couldn't you do what he asked? You are a pathetic excuse for a mother!"

"I did not choose Bernie," Ruth insisted. She told me she had planned to tell her sons just that week that she was finished with their father, even though she still didn't really see why it mattered. "Well, I guess I'm too late," she added.

"Ruth." I seethed, needing to hurt her, to make her acknowledge, for once, the damage she had done. "Your son is dead, and as far as I'm concerned, I'm dead to you, too, and Audrey and Nick are, too. You will *never* see your grandchildren again and you will never see me again!" I stomped back inside. Marty and Rob stood in the dining room, their mouths agape at what they'd heard.

"How'd you like *that*?" I said, still shaking. Yes, it was cruel to speak that way to a woman who had just lost her son, but I needed desperately to defend him. Becoming Mark's avenger had seamlessly become part of my own personality. I wanted to lay blame, demand accountability, and keen out loud in the pain he could not endure.

Bernie's lawyer issued a pompous statement announcing that Bernie would not be seeking permission from his jailors to attend his son's funeral. I was nauseated by the thought.

RoseMarie, Christi, and I went to the grocery store to buy food for the mourners. The three of us were in a daze, wandering the aisles trying to find paper plates and figure out how many plastic forks we might need. Just a few weeks before, Mark and I had been shopping for our Saturday night dinner in the same store, trying to decide whether to roast a chicken or make some pasta. I remembered how we had taken our glasses of wine to the backyard after putting the kids down for the night. We lit a fire in the copper fire pit and sat quietly talking about our future. Now I pushed my cart aimlessly through the aisles and felt as if I were narrating a documentary about some sad woman I didn't recognize.

It was surreal to be doing these things. *I am shopping for food for my husband's memorial service,* I told my disbelieving self. How did people go from the aisles of the A&P to a loved one's grave? Was there some secret gear I was missing that allows you to shift smoothly from whole to shattered and then back to whole again? RoseMarie had made meatballs. I put cheese and crackers in the shopping cart. I didn't want there to be food or drink. This wasn't a social event. I didn't want anyone to linger. I wanted to just get through this service and have it be over.

On the day of the memorial, I dressed myself in a black sweater and pants. I told Audrey that a lot of people were going to come visit that evening because they missed Daddy a lot, too. I decided not to force the children to sit through the service, but to let them be there if they wandered in out of curiosity. We would say our own private good-byes to Daddy later. This wasn't a funeral or a wake. There would be no maudlin, blown-up photos of Mark smiling back at us, no shrine, no hymns, no minister or prayers. His ashes in their black box sat discreetly on a marble end table surrounded by photos of the four children and me.

There were twenty-five, maybe thirty of us in all. I sat in a chair off to the side, with my mother kneeling next to me and my aunt on an ottoman in front of me, my mom rubbing my back, my aunt clasping my hands in hers. I can't bear being singled out for attention, good or bad. I hate it when people sing "Happy Birthday" to me. I felt deeply ashamed of what my husband had done, embarrassed for him. Bernie had shown him all too clearly the power a father has to crush his children, yet now he had done the same to his.

The hurt Mark had caused me I might someday forgive. But I couldn't imagine ever forgiving what he did to Nicholas, Audrey, Kate, and Daniel. He had gone to such extremes to be there, always, for Kate and Daniel, only to rip that security away from them in an instant. Audrey wouldn't have him even for as long as his older children had, and Nick would know his father now only through the memories of others. In ending his own life, Mark had irrevocably altered the course of theirs. Kate was a fifteen-year-old high school sophomore and competitive swimmer who had grown up hearing her father cheer from the bleachers. Daniel was an eighteen-year-old freshman at college, sampling independence for the first time. Even the occasional one-line text messages he sent from college would make Mark's face break into a happy, loopy grin. Now Daniel and Kate huddled together, waiting their turns to eulogize their father while a cousin played with Nick and Audrey in the other room.

I had asked Mark's friends Joe and Adam to speak, along with Andy, my brother Rob, Kate, and Daniel. I began to sob and couldn't stop, all their words mostly lost on me as warm tears flooded down my face. I remember Andy saying something about feeling bitter and angry before he said something loving about his brother. Catherine perched on the couch. We managed to avoid each other, but she made a point of walking up to Rob's wife, Sloane, greeting my sister-in-law with a sarcastic joke. "Hi, Stephanie," she sang, alluding to a tabloid photo that had misidentified Sloane, on the day of Mark's suicide, as me.

Kate shared the sweet memory of her dad calling out after her, "Hey, Kate! Learn a lot!" whenever he dropped her off at school. Daniel stood up to speak as the brief service drew to a close.

"I just want to say I want everyone to get along," was all he said.

My wedding rings came off when I went to bed that night, and never went back on.

That night, Mark appeared in another dream. He was sitting in the same chair I had sat in during the service, but again, I could see his face only in profile, as if he were half there, half not. A single tear was coursing down his cheek. I woke up feeling certain he regretted what he had done to all of us. I'm not a religious or mystical person, but I am utterly certain that his spirit is sometimes present still. It happens in waking hours, too. I will sense but not see him suddenly beside me, filling an empty space.

Those of us he left behind keep trying, in our miserable, dysfunctional way, to be there for one another and live up to the challenge Daniel voiced at the memorial service, but old habits are hard to break. It took only a day for me to feel that I was being deceived yet again. "Have you ever woken up and you're not sure whether you were dreaming or somebody really told you something?" I asked Marty as we went out for coffee the morning after the service. "I think somebody told me Ruth was at Susan's."

"Why don't you call and ask?" Marty suggested. I sent a text message to Debbie Madoff, Andy's wife, who was a close friend of Susan's. Mark and I had felt sorry for Debbie following Bernie's arrest; as Andy's legal wife and mother of his two daughters, her finances were tangled in the same legal web as ours, and her isolation from the family made the uncertainty all that much worse. We had kept her updated via occasional e-mails, and she had come by and been sweetly supportive since Mark's death. I texted her from the Dunkin' Donuts parking lot. *Is it true Ruth has been staying at Susan's?*

A reply popped up instantly. *I'm not going to get involved. You should give her a call.*

Susan answered on the first ring.

"Hey, is Ruth at your house?" I asked, trying to sound casual and hoping it had, in fact, been a troubling dream.

Susan answered with an invective rant so loud I had to hold the phone away from my ear. Marty couldn't help but hear every word; he looked at me in surprise. "You're doing what you think is right for your kids, and I'm doing what I think is right for my kids!" Susan yelled. "The kids need their grandmother. They want her here!"

I hung up, dismayed that I was being lambasted by her yet again. So much for openness and honesty. How could she have sat there at my dining table offering her help while playing secret hostess the entire time to the woman she knew I held partly accountable for Mark's death? I assumed that Susan hadn't been forthcoming because she had feared I would disinvite her from the memorial service if I knew Ruth was staying with her. But she had missed my point entirely: I just wanted everyone to be up-front for once. At the end of the day, I truly didn't care whether she became Ruth's biggest cheerleader or her worst enemy. Just own it. No more secrets. No more playing both sides against the middle. No more lies.

What Susan and I did have in common was an overpowering determination to protect our children from further hurt, and to help them cope with the loss of their father as best as we could. Because of that, we tried to put the Ruth incident behind us for their sakes and lurch forward in our clumsy new alliance. I wanted us to remain in one another's lives so Kate's and Daniel's little brother and sister could grow up knowing them, and knowing their father through their eyes as well. I was deeply touched when Daniel and his stepfather showed up one day with a Christmas tree for me. Even though he was Jewish and, at eighteen, far too cool to get excited over my silly stockings,

Daniel knew how much the holiday had always meant to me, and he realized that someone had better start making the funereal house festive for the sake of Nick and Audrey.

The tree he had chosen was a weird lollipop shape that made me laugh, and I decided that he had struck the perfect note: Whimsy was the only way to get through this holiday. If I tried to replicate the Hallmark-worthy Christmas I usually put on, the horror of what Mark had done and the loss of him would only be underscored. I wanted the exact opposite of what I would have had with Mark. During one of their runs back and forth to the city, my brother and sister-in-law drove up with the gifts I had already bought, but I asked them not to bring up my collection of ornaments or our stockings. Mark had always gotten a kick out of decorating the tree with me, and we had both loved watching Audrey's delight the year before as she discovered the beautiful baubles and special treasures like the pom-pom ice-cream cone ornament my aunt had made. Now Rob and I headed to the mall to buy cheesy colored lights, tinsel, and cheap ornaments for our lollipop tree. I wanted to be able to throw away everything when it was over, to have no reminders of the Christmas Mark took his life. I didn't want a sad tree.

I picked out a miniature plastic bottle of Pinot Grigio with tiny plastic grapes, and another ornament shaped like a wedge of Brie—every night, people had been coming over to visit, and we'd fallen into the habit of an hors d'oeuvres hour. I got Dora the Explorer, Disney princesses, and other cartoon characters for the kids, and briefly contemplated a huge inflatable snowman or Santa for the yard.

Browsing the Christmas store with Rob, I would go from laughing at a blue-cheese ornament one minute to numb again the next. I would feel Mark there laughing next to me, and then I would find myself alone again in an empty moment while waiting for the machine to process my credit card, or for the clerk to hand me my bags. To this day, I still can't lie down and take a nap, because it's an empty moment. Those are the hardest. It doesn't matter whether it's two hours or two minutes. It's those moments when my imagination takes cruel flight and I visualize the last two hours, the last two minutes, of my husband's life.

I had the same feeling on Christmas that I'd had the day of Mark's memorial: I just wanted it to be done. Over. I felt forced into putting on the show for everyone else; just canceling it altogether had crossed my mind, but there was no way I could do that to my kids. I would have to fake my way through it for them. As soon as everyone got their stockings on Christmas morning—I had bought cheap red felt ones at the mall and inscribed each name with glitter glue—I tossed them out. (Audrey, it turned out, loved hers, and had a major meltdown when she couldn't find it—we had to go dig it out of the trash can.) I also got rid of every gift I received that day, even the bracelet my parents gave me, because I didn't want to remember that time. Mark had shopped for Kate and Daniel online, and I had wrapped the clothes and other gifts he ordered back when they arrived. We all went through the rote motions of opening gifts and exclaiming over them. No one was happy that day.

In the afternoon, I put out a spread of appetizers, including

Daniel's favorite mini hot dogs, which he left untouched. Once I'd put everything away, the kids announced they were hungry and started making frozen pizzas. I knew they were hurting as much as I was, and I hated myself for silently feeling resentful. Later, my mother heated up the two huge lasagnas we had brought from a nearby Italian restaurant. Carrying one of the pans to the table, she dropped the whole thing over the back of a wicker chair and burst into tears. "Just throw the chair out!" I snapped rudely. "How am I going to get that out?" My sister-in-law, Sloane, quickly removed the slipcover and washed it, and we picked at the salvaged lasagna.

"Steph, do you mind if I go out tonight to meet my friends?" Daniel ventured to ask as we sat later in the living room.

"No, of course not, go ahead, have fun," I told him. "Just wake me when you get home so I know you're safe," I added, stunned to hear Mark's words suddenly coming out of my mouth.

"I don't want to take my car," Daniel announced. "I want to take the Denali." Mark had gotten us the black extended SUV just before Nick was born. "In fact," Daniel went on, "I want that car for school."

My parents and I were startled. Mark had bought his son a brand-new car less than a year ago. Now I handed him my keys and stammered out a weak reply, knowing how hard the day must have been for him, too. I couldn't blame him for acting out over such a minor issue.

"I can't guarantee anything," I said. "Just be safe tonight."

When our sad little Christmas was over and I was tossing out the crumpled wrapping paper, I discovered the store-generated gift cards Daniel had found tucked in with his new shirts and had quietly left behind: *To Daniel, Merry Christmas, love Dad and Steph.* I felt awful that he had seen that, and blamed myself for being such an idiot and not thinking to look for any cards. Betrayed first by his grandfather and now abandoned by his own father, poor Daniel was growing too accustomed to life dealing him painful surprises. I hated being any part of that.

I had no real plan for what we would do after the holidays. I had vowed never to return to Mercer Street. My brother and stepfather would get whatever I needed out of the apartment, and I could easily shift our lives to Greenwich until I figured out what to do next. But after a few weeks in Connecticut, I began to have second thoughts. The outpouring of love and support from our little neighborhood community back in SoHo had been tremendous. Citibabes, where Nick and Audrey took art and music classes, sent a favorite teacher up to spend some time playing her guitar and singing with them. Ella and Scarlett came up with their mothers to play with Audrey one day and brought thoughtful gifts for me and the kids.

Classmates from grad school had reached out, too. I had never used my married name with these new friends, and had pretty carefully hidden my connection to the infamous Bernard Madoff, even flipping the mail on our hall table facedown before answering the door when they stopped by to visit. School had been the one place I could escape to where my life didn't revolve around the Ponzi scheme, and I treasured those four hours of anonymity a week. It turned out that I had fooled most, but not everyone. Anyone Googling my maiden name could quickly connect the dots, but not even the people who had met Mark and socialized with us ever said a word. Discovering how kindly they had respected my privacy made me treasure those fledgling friendships even more. It dawned on me that I would be making a big mistake to cut myself off now from a network of support that made me feel so safe and loved. My kids needed to regain their sense of normalcy and stability, too. And I wasn't going to obsess over the media the way my husband had.

Dodging the press was the least of my concerns now. I had gotten that out of my system with a therapeutic exercise one cold and foggy night in Greenwich after everyone else was asleep. Designed for pediatric patients at the hospital, it involves drawing a target of whatever a patient fears most—a doctor, maybe, or a big needle—and then pelting it with wads of wet toilet paper. That night in Greenwich, I made myself a stockpile of "soggies" and crept into the woods shielding our house from the street. Hiding behind the trees, I began lobbing my missiles at the few media cars still parked on the road. I could hear the surprised cries of "Hey! What was that?" before engines started and they drove away. I laughed like a lunatic in the frozen woods. I had always wanted to do something like that. The childish impulse first rose when we sought refuge in Connecticut after Bernie's arrest. I told Mark we should pull some prank on the press stakeout. We had life-sized cutouts of Ruth and Bernie up in the attic, left over from some family celebration or birthday party. I desperately wanted to prop them up at the end of the driveway. "Don't," Mark had admonished. He should have let me do it, and he should have done it with me. It felt so good to have even a fleeting sense of control.

On New Year's Eve, I decided I could face going back to SoHo. The kids were homesick. They missed their scooters and their toys. They wanted to see their friends and go to the Jamba Juice on the corner again, and watch *Night at the Museum* over and over and over.

Stepping into my apartment building's small lobby with my parents, kids, and Grouper, I dreaded facing the doorman and his pity. *What* do *you say to me,* I thought, *how* do *you act around me?* In the elevator, I thought of my husband being carried out in a body bag, the stretcher trundling out onto the sidewalk and up to the coroner's van. The elevator's discreet *ding* announced that we had arrived on our floor. The door opened directly into our loft, and I walked into the foyer and looked up at the fresh plaster and paint used to camouflage the steel beam where Mark had hanged himself. I bolted to the bathroom and threw up.

I went into our bedroom and stared at the bed. My side was perfectly made, but Mark's had been pulled back. I could tell that he had lain but not slept there; the sheets and pillow were unwrinkled. No suicide notes had been found, but I still couldn't believe that the few one-line e-mails we got at Disney World were all there was. I rooted through the nightstand and searched the closet. I opened the door of the medicine cabinet, thinking maybe he had hidden an explanation there. There was none. There were no pills missing, no evidence Mark had even had a drink that night. I found a pair of his socks in the hamper and held them to my face, trying to find the scent of him and crying when it wasn't there. On the day he went back to college, Daniel had taken some of his father's clothes and shoes from our closet in

Connecticut while I was out, and the shirt I had been sleeping in was gone when I went to put it on that night. I didn't want to ask for it back, and the intimacy of it would no longer be there, anyway. But now I had lost the smell of Mark.

The black box containing his ashes was in a Whole Foods tote in the hallway with our luggage, alongside the new vacuum cleaner my mother had bought to replace the one with the gruesomely snapped cord. Other things would have to be replaced as well. I ordered a new mattress. I needed new sheets, too. Mark and I had always had snowy white ones. Now I got an Indian print in bright pink and orange and lime green, the brightest, happiest colors I could find. I threw out all the coffee and switched to tea. I got a stepladder and climbed up to inspect the repaired beam. I found faint scuff marks on the ceiling, with matching ones on the wood floor directly below. *This is where,* I told myself. It was the same spot where he had hung Audrey's birthday piñata barely a month before.

In bed alone at night, I began waking up drenched in sweat, my heart racing. I stared at the clock, waiting for 4:14 to come. The time stamp on Mark's final e-mails. I knew he had to have done it right after. Watching the minutes tick by, my mind conjured every horrific detail. How high up was he, what was he wearing, was it quick, did it hurt, was he crying? I put my hands around my own throat and squeezed, trying to imagine what it felt like to strangle the last breath of air from your lungs.

I can't be here, I told myself. *I don't know how I'm going to live here. I can't stay. I can't be here.*

nine

OUR OWN GOOD-BYE

I never did find any note or explanation from Mark beyond that last e-mail he sent the morning he hanged himself, nothing but the words *I Love You*. I have my own theories about why he took his life and what he hoped it would accomplish. They're only guesses, of course, and intellectually, I know better than to try to apply reason to such an irrational act. Emotionally is a different story. But I am sure of this one small, comforting truth: He never did this thinking for a moment that his torment would become mine.

Everyone who was suing Bernie Madoff's son when he was alive kept suing him when he was dead. What Mark and I had been facing together I now face alone, with no job, no income of my own, and two young children to raise. Resolving Mark's estate has added new complications to a financial minefield, and it's anyone's guess as to when there will be closure there. I had decided to go back to school right away, enrolling in just one class, but emotionally I felt paralyzed, unable to make even simple decisions some days, like whether to meet a friend for coffee.

Our babysitter, Petal, and Mark's friend Joe had been the last ones to see my husband alive, other than the doorman who exchanged pleasantries with Mark when he took Grouper out for his usual evening stroll. Mark and Joe had met for lunch earlier that Friday, and Joe would remember Mark laughing and enjoying himself. He told me that Mark was excited that Audrey and I would be coming home from Disney World the following day. How had he spiraled downward so soon, so fast, after such a pleasant, innocuous afternoon? Mark's oldest friend, Adam, had also seen him that day, and noticed nothing out of the ordinary. I can only pinpoint the *Wall Street Journal* article and the new lawsuit against the children as the forces that pushed him over the edge that particular day. With his death, I believe he wanted to make a statement to his father. I also think he had convinced himself we would be better off without him. Nothing makes me angrier, or sadder.

Since Mark's death, I've browsed books and articles about suicide, skimming the surface, afraid to absorb too much information for fear I will use it to condemn myself. People assume that the loved ones left behind after a suicide yearn to know why, but that's not my main obsession. *What if?* That's the question I ask myself again and again, trying on and discarding every possibility. What if I hadn't gone to

Disney World, what if I had pretended not to be annoyed by his rant about the *Wall Street Journal*, what if I had woken up and checked my e-mail at 4:14, what if I had never met him, never loved him, never lost him? There are people who never knew Mark Madoff, yet who gleefully point to his suicide as proof that he must have known of or participated in his father's epic crime. Nothing could be further from the truth. His death was proof only of his pain.

I've since learned that approximately half the people who kill themselves in this country each year have tried it before, and are most likely to try it again during the first year following the failed attempt. No one who treated Mark after he swallowed the pills told me that, and I ask myself constantly whether I missed something, whether my vigilance might have countered his vulnerability. Then I have to remind myself that what I saw that winter was a man who seemed hopeful and happy for the first time since his world had caved in on December 11, 2008. Mark had stopped taking antidepressants several months after leaving the psych ward in 2009, saying he no longer needed them, but he was still seeing a therapist. So was I. To be sure, the stress factors were still there—Mark's nervous habit of scratching his palm would sometimes leave the tender patch of flesh between his thumb and forefinger raw and bleeding—but our marriage was getting stronger, to the point that we were even talking about having a third child.

Mark's greatest fear, beyond being unjustly accused and destroyed both professionally and financially, was that I would leave rather than

weather the storm with him. He had never known anything but priv-
ilege, and he lacked the basic tools to cope with any adversity, much
less this monumental one. Even his divorce had caused only mini-
mal disruption to his comfortable life. When Bernie confessed,
Mark's world collapsed in a heap on top of him. He couldn't manage
to free himself, much less begin building anew. His father, his mother,
and his brother had all turned their backs on him in some way
or another, and when his paranoia got the better of him, Mark assumed I was going to abandon him, too, despite my reassurances
that I wouldn't. Once, as he was standing at the island in our kitchen
ruminating over some lawsuit or press report attacking his integrity again, he suddenly blurted out that the kids and I would probably be better off without him. I remember running across the room
and flinging myself at him, sobbing like a crazy woman as I hugged
him tight.

"Please don't say that! It's not true! Please, please, don't ever say
that!" I begged him.

There was a tacit understanding between us that I would never
bring up his overdose. I knew Mark was deeply embarrassed by it, and
he had apologized in the love letter he had written me from his hospital bed. He had promised me he would never do anything like that
again, and I believed him. I never opened the medicine cabinet to
count pills. I never looked through his belongings, his pockets, his
correspondence, for evidence of his despair. Nick and Audrey were
proof enough of their father's will to live, I thought, because even in

his darkest moments, Mark had never ceased to be an attentive, ador-
ing father. He could be sucked into the Internet whirlpool, wallowing
in self-pity and anger, then calmly get up when it was time to bathe
the kids, put a towel over his head, and lose himself in their giggles as
he roared, "The Towel Monster is going to get you!"

Driving along the Henry Hudson Parkway one gorgeous fall
afternoon on our way home from Greenwich, Mark and I had talked
about the day when optics would no longer rule our life and we would
finally be free to tell our own story. It was going to be about love,
betrayal, and survival. About righting your ship, finding the horizon,
and setting the course to sail back to safe harbor. Mark had started
fiddling with an opening chapter two weeks before he died. He never
got past these first few paragraphs.

After forty-four years of life, I found out that my father was
not the person that I knew. On December 10, the man who had
taught me the importance of integrity had just told me that he
was a thief. It's unclear exactly when it started, but it appears
as if I was a young boy when his lies began. The business, the
man, the person that I so looked up to, was not who or what
he claimed to be. Yet somehow, my father was able to leave the

fraudulent side of his life on the seventeenth floor of his office and come home to his children and be a good father. That is the person that I knew. That is the person his family knew. That is the person that his friends knew. My childhood was normal. I was taught right from wrong. Both of my parents were always there for me and both helped make me into the person that I am today. I was raised to be, and still am, a good and honest person.

I lived in awe of my father from a very young age. He was the man that everyone wanted to be. His business was successful; he had the admiration of his colleagues and the respect of government officials. But it was more than simple praise. To us, it felt like constant glorification from heads of business, regulatory bodies, and exchanges. I knew my father to be one of the leaders of Wall Street, not a master criminal. I knew my father, yet the person he is now was not he.

I am the son of a crook. I am also a son, and a son looks up to their father from day one. My father taught me to throw a baseball, he taught me to be a good husband, and he taught me to be a good father to my own children. I saw him as a great man. As I got older and grew professionally, the aura surrounding my father only grew. For my entire professional life, I worked diligently to build a business that would make my father proud. Bernard Madoff was one of the most respected men on Wall Street and he was my father. How could he be a crook? Ironically, I grew up fearful that I would always find myself in my father's shadow, never being able to known [sic] for what I myself had achieved. I wanted so badly to be the person that my father was . . . and now I can't get far enough away.

I lived a big life by Main Street standards. Wall Street had been my home for my entire career and I had achieved a lot. My future, as I had known it, looked bright. My market making business was peaking in profitability and my proprietary trading desk was close to even, dramatically outperforming the indexes. I was proud of what I had done. While the horrors of my father's deception will cast a broad shadow, what I had accomplished professionally was significant. I will not allow that to be forgotten.

I have read that there are those that feel since my father was bad, I must be bad or at least must have known that he was.

Why, because I was his son? My father stole from his brother, sister, niece, nephew, best friends, coworkers, and countless others. Somehow, he was able to disguise his true character from them. It should not come as a surprise that the one who idolized him the most, his son, would not see his own father as a criminal. My father was a wolf in sheep's clothing. He was not the man that anyone thought that he was.

My own father has stolen my life from me. It's pain that is beyond description. The business that I spent twenty-three years building gone, I am unemployed, my livelihood destroyed, and my family will forever live with the shame of what my father has done. There were so many victims of my father's fraud, so many horrible stories. How do I explain to my children what I do not understand myself?

How do I explain this to them? I ask Mark still, as Nick and Audrey chase each other past the candle I keep burning, like an eternal flame, in the foyer. The women who came to do a spiritual cleansing of the apartment placed it there and told me to keep it lit at all times, but the thought that it might set something on fire while we sleep scares me. So I whisper a small "Sorry" and blow it out each night, smiling, because Mark was such a worrywart, and I know he would approve.

The cleansing was a gift from my friend Mariana. Mercer Street is a small, cobblestoned lane, but the upscale façades of retail stores and boutiques belie an old-fashioned neighborliness among the regulars who work and live there. Everyone, from the manager of our favorite restaurant on the corner to the young manicurists who worked in the nail salon two doors down, was anxious to know how I was doing after Mark's suicide; comforting words trickled back to me via the urban grapevine, from my babysitter or dog walker or doorman. The familiarity of my neighborhood was what had drawn me back from my lonely grief in Greenwich, but once home, I felt too embarrassed to show my face. I was ashamed of what Mark had done, afraid to face the inevitable questions and concerned looks. I could never tell when the tears were going to suddenly flow, and I hated the thought of breaking down in public.

My mom was getting her nails done one day soon afterward at Haven, the little salon next door to my apartment building, where I was a regular and knew all the employees by name. Mariana, a hip and pretty young Mexican manicurist, wanted my mother to ask me about having my apartment spiritually cleansed. I was raised by a Catholic mother and a Jewish stepfather, but I'm not a religious person. I seized upon Mariana's suggestion hungrily. This was exactly what I needed! The place felt haunted, and the fear and anger I was carrying only added to the oppressive atmosphere inside a space that used to be so bright and airy. I eagerly accepted Mariana's offer, not knowing what to expect, but open to any possibility.

Mariana issued her instructions: First, I was to keep a clear glass bowl of cold water behind the front door, changing it every twenty-four hours and checking it for a week before the cleanse. "Negative energy will make it bubble up," she said. I did as she told me, and the very next morning the water was fizzing like club soda. I changed the water, and the same thing happened again.

Mariana arrived at nine o'clock on the appointed morning with Karen, a Colombian woman with a friendly face and calming presence, who gently but firmly took charge. The pair began unloading the bags they had brought with them and set up a little shrine on a table in the foyer, placing a fat candle on a circle of royal blue satin, then arranging smaller candles around it. They changed into simple white skirts and blouses and wrapped their heads in white cotton scarves. This was for protection from negative energy, they explained.

Mariana had instructed me to have the children out of the apartment during the cleanse, but told me I would need to stay during the ritual.

"You'll have a reaction, but it will be healing," she explained now, warning me that I would likely start to cry.

"Some people behave like a baby," Karen added, noting that some even lose control of their bladders.

I was terrified. What were these women going to do to me? Was I going to slip into some trance, or enter a mind-altering state I couldn't escape? I wanted to summon Demi Moore in *Ghost*, not Linda Blair in *The Exorcist*. The prospect of breaking down in front of these two women, no matter how kind, made me nervous.

"Do the apartment, not me," I said.

No, they insisted, they had to do both, or it wouldn't work. They gave me a cloth and told me to wrap my head and stand where Mark had died. From their bags, they pulled out a conch shell, charcoal, and solidified sap from a tree in Mexico. They lit the sap and charcoal in a ceramic bowl. A piney scent reminiscent of myrrh filled the air, and they began chanting in soft Spanish. Karen stood in front of me, Mariana behind me.

"Take deep breaths, then blow it all out," Mariana urged, exhaling a heavy sigh to show me how. She rubbed my shoulders and back to calm me.

"You're safe," Karen said. "You're going to be safe."

Karen moved the bowl of sap and charcoal in circular motions, letting the smoke waft in my face, while sprinkling me with fragrant water. I kept my eyes closed through most of the ritual. Mariana held the conch to her lips and began to blow it like a horn, its sound low and mournful, and I began to cry.

My cleansing complete, Karen and Mariana started in on the apartment, going from south to east, to north, then west, dousing all three of us periodically with the scented water, for protection, they said. First, they cleansed the children's room, climbing on furniture and crouching into corners to get the smoke into every possible crevice. Then they moved to my room, where both Karen and Mariana focused their energies primarily on my bed, standing in the center of it, then pulling the covers back to smoke out my pillows. In my closet, Karen spotted Mark's clothes still hanging on the rods and insisted on cleansing me again. I stood there among his empty suits and crisp shirts and felt the tears flood my face, uncontrollable, and I wept as I had never wept before.

We covered every inch of the rest of the house with smoke from the burning sap. Mariana and Karen wanted me to clap as they chanted, but I felt too self-conscious, so they found a tambourine among the kids' toys and let me use that instead. For three hours, we inched our way through every room, until smoke filled the house thick as fog. Twice, the smoke alarms went off and I had to race to open the big windows overlooking Mercer Street. By the time it was all over, Karen and Mariana were both spent, drenched in perspiration, chugging bottles of water. We opened the front door to let the negative energy out. They changed back into their street clothes, hugged me, and reminded me to keep the glass bowl of water by the front door. Mariana had to go to work, but Karen hung back. I decided to test her.

"I find it really interesting that you put it here," I said, nodding toward the small shrine with its candle still glowing. Neither she nor Mariana had ever been in the apartment before, and I hadn't spoken about the significance of that spot. "Why did you do that?" I asked.

"Because I could feel that this was where he died," she answered matter-of-factly. The candle flickered directly below the beam—since concealed—where Mark had hanged himself.

That night, I sat in the window seat where Mark used to go to try to clear his head, and I looked out at the starless city night. "I forgive you," I said. "I forgive you for leaving us." In that moment, I physically felt my anger dissolve, and sorrow take its place.

I was shocked by how much harder it is to be sad.

In Greenwich, sleep had been my refuge in the weeks immediately following Mark's death. There were always family members or friends in the house to keep an eye on the kids, and I would retreat to my bed when I needed to just lie down and let the sadness wash over me. Back in SoHo, though, anxiety joined forces with my sorrow, and sleep came only in short, fevered jags, ending with my ritual panic attack as the hour of Mark's death drew near each night. Barely a month after losing him, I wandered into the kitchen at four a.m., unable to sleep. I sat at the kitchen counter and began writing Bernie Madoff a bitter letter.

Bernie—

I find it strange that I am the one to be writing you a condolence letter—but there is no question in my mind that the reason I can write to you is because I have more manners, bravery, and certainly more dignity than you—so perhaps this letter should not arrive to you as that much of a shock.

That being said, I have heard there is no greater pain than losing a child, and for that I am sorry for the loss of your son.

Up until the day he died, Mark always made me feel very happy and, most importantly, he made me feel very loved. He gave me two beautiful children that get me out of bed in the morning and give me a reason for living.

I understand that you stole money from thousands of innocent people—your children, your grandchildren, your entire family, and even my parents. However, what you must know is that you stole the love of my life and four of your grandchildren's father. You stole something from me that can never be replaced. You stole Mark—a loving husband, devoted father, and my best friend.

I deserve an explanation from you as to why and how you as a human being can possibly live knowing how much pain and destruction you have caused. I deserve an explanation as to how you feel about Mark's death—or do you even have any feelings?

I pray that your days in jail are as dark as they can be, because let me tell you, it's much harder to survive on the outside—and I refuse to let you ruin my life.

Stephanie

As I signed what I knew would be my last letter to Bernie Madoff, the aroma of fresh-brewed coffee filled the kitchen. I glanced at the clock; Mark would be getting up now. Making coffee had always been his ritual, and the scent would wake me each morning. I hadn't made a pot since he died. Now I inhaled the incredible smell deeply, comforted by it, taking it as a sign that this letter to his father was the right thing to do. The water in the bowl by the front door remained still and clear.

Not long after that, I had one of those dreams where you fight consciousness as it pulls you back to the surface because you can't bear to wake up and have it all end. Mark had come to me again, and crawled into bed beside me. He hugged me, and we were both laughing hysterically. But then it was time for me to take Audrey to school, and I begged him not to leave, to wait for me to come back. When I reached the bedroom door and looked back, he was already disappearing. I woke up feeling as if it had been a gift; we had gotten to spend time together again. A few days later, an envelope turned up in my mail bearing the prison's return address. Bernie had written back.

I pray that you never have to experience the pain and torment I live with every day. I would gladly give my own life if I thought it would bring Mark back . . . I blame myself for everything that has happened and nothing will ever change this . . . You ask how I can live with myself. I can't, and I don't know how much longer I can go on.

He signed it *Love, Bernie,* and added a postscript, imploring me to let Ruth back into my life.

you also said that it is harder for you outside. It's not my problem. It's My environment in here is living with myself and the torment of every waking moment. *Bernie*

Stephanie,
I have not stopped thinking about your I had to add something. I'm sure Mark

1-19-

Dear Stephanie,

BERNARD MADOFF 61727-054
Name: Number:
Federal Correctional Institution
P.O. Box 1000
Butner, NC 27509

Stephani

sent to Butner which is considered to be the best and most layback prison in It has the look and feel of a college campus with lovely lawns and trees. I in a dorm (one story) with 24 other guys with plenty of privacy. I can go to go pretty much as I please with no lock ups. I hope a clerks job and everyone treats me with respect and friendship. I have loads of to every right in S. As you can would fit right in. most are covered with Mafia Don's the celebrity and

①

Stephanie,
you are absolutely right. There is no pa greater than losing a child. From the day Mark was born I have loved him more than life itself. He gave me nothing but

Dear Stephanie,
thank you for your lovely letter
It meant so much to me. Hearing about
The children and

Bernie

Stephanie, I can only ask you to try and remember the love you witnessed between me and all of you.

Love,
Bernie

P.S.
Stephanie
Ruth has little to live for other than our family. You know she loves you and I

It was very difficult to give me up after a life of 55 years together, *which she has now done,* he claimed. I shook my head in disgust as I read it. The lies, it seemed, would never stop.

Even as he supposedly poured out his heart to me on a lined legal pad, Bernie was granting select reporters prison interviews, basking in the attention, and even joking about his newfound appreciation for Danielle Steel romance novels. "I am a good person," he told *New York* magazine. His narcissism might have been laughable had it not been so dangerous. Mark was the fourth known suicide linked to Bernie's crime. A French financier had slit his wrist with a box cutter and bled to death in his office. A British investor shot himself, and another Madoff victim had hanged himself in a London hotel room.

Mark's memorial in Greenwich had been a fiasco, full of tension, lies, and distrust. It was not how I wanted to say good-bye. I didn't want to keep him in the black metal box on my nightstand forever, either. I planned to scatter some of his ashes in places that had been meaningful to us, and I wanted to do that by myself. I planned to take just a small portion of the remains and leave the rest for Mark's four children and brother to have when they felt ready to say their own good-byes, in their own ways. The funeral director graciously offered to help me.

"How long will this take?" I asked as I reluctantly handed over the black metal box. "I'm kind of nervous to spend the night away from him." My eyes were no doubt red and swollen. Mr. Kuhn looked at me sympathetically.

"No longer than twenty-four hours," he gently assured me, adding, "I'm so sorry." I left and started wandering the neighborhood in a daze. I had a parent-teacher conference at Audrey's school in a few hours, but felt too anxious and unsettled to go back home with the empty shopping bag I had used to carry the black box uptown. On Second Avenue, I passed a movie theater and bought a ticket to *The Fighter*. When I came back out, my phone rang. The funeral director had compassionately given my request priority, and the remains were ready to be picked up again. I hurried back to the funeral home and picked up the black box still containing most of Mark's remains and six smaller containers, each the size of a ring box. Inside each little box, two teaspoons of ash were sealed in a plastic packet.

By now, I was running late for the teacher conference, so I left my SoulCycle bag with its precious contents in the lobby with my doorman and rushed to the school. I nodded and smiled in the appropriate places as the three teachers showed me Audrey's work and told me how great she was, and how well she seemed to be handling it all. *It*, I had learned, is the best euphemism we have for suicide. I flipped through the portfolio of Audrey's work and stopped when I saw a drawing of a flower. *For Dada*, she had written neatly across the top. I thought I had already cried myself dry for the day, but now I was blinking back yet more tears.

"I can't believe I'm here alone," was all I could say.

My parents had invited us to spend a week at their home in St. Barths, and I took a little box of Mark's ashes with me. He hated being cold, and the warm Caribbean beach was his idea of paradise. Mr. Kuhn had asked me if I planned on taking any of the remains on board a plane.

"Can I make the suggestion that you be forthcoming with security?" he said.

"I'm going to put it in my luggage," I explained. Bathing suits, flip-flops, sunscreen, Daddy. When widowhood wasn't tragic, it was ludicrous. There seemed to be no in-between.

"No, don't do that," the funeral director admonished. It would raise suspicions on an X-ray or hand search. "They may confiscate."

"But it has his name on it," I objected. The boxes were clearly labeled. That label was exactly why I wasn't about to disclose the contents and take it through with my carry-on. It had been barely two months since the suicide was on the front page of every New York paper. I didn't want WIDOW SNEAKING ASHES OUT OF COUNTRY to be the next tabloid headline.

I ended up taking my chances, packing the little box, and I was not forthcoming with security. I sailed through without a problem.

As much as I wanted my own farewell and some sense that I was giving Mark a resting place he would have wanted, I also dreaded this moment. At Gouverneur Beach—Mark's favorite beach in the world—my parents hung back as I crossed the sand to the spot where we had always put down our towels. I walked into the warm sea until I was waist-deep and sprinkled the gritty remains into the water. I was shocked when they instantly sank. I waded back to shore, and my parents wrapped me in their arms, and the three of us cried. This sadness felt different, though. It was a peaceful sadness.

March came before I knew it, before I was ready. Mark's birthday was March 11. He would have been forty-seven. The thought, again, of a forced family get-together overwhelmed me. In spite of my love for them, my relationship with Kate and Daniel had become undefined. And the relationship between Andy and me was strained at best. The only time he had even contacted me since his brother's death had been two months later, in February, when he called me around Nick's birthday and angrily demanded to know whether I was planning to write a book. He had heard rumors from someone he would not name.

"Yes," I told him. I wanted to tell my story, "and I want to give your brother a voice."

"Well, I am sure it must be nice for you to finally get noticed and get some attention," he sneered. "I am sure that must feel good to you."

"Not really," I answered truthfully. This was something I needed to do for my children, and for Mark. I didn't understand why Andy wouldn't want vindication for his tormented brother, too.

We had no further contact until just before Mark's birthday, when Andy sent an e-mail out of the blue saying he wanted to come by. I was just leaving St. Barths. I sent an e-mail back explaining that I was about to get on a plane and wouldn't be home until late that night.

I don't want you to think I am blowing you off or making excuses to not get together, I replied. *I am just traveling a lot these couple of weeks. Also, just out of curiosity . . . why all of the sudden interest to see me and the kids?* He had never paid any attention to his niece and nephew before, and hadn't asked about them since their father died.

I want to have a relationship with Audrey and Nick, and as Mark's birthday approaches I've been thinking about it a lot, he answered, adding that his schedule was flexible. I responded that I planned to get away for Mark's birthday. I didn't volunteer where I was going.

I decided to just escape and spend a few days in Nantucket with Nick and Audrey. I planned to take my remaining share of Mark's ashes with me to scatter. "I don't think you should do this alone," my brother, Rob, said when I told him my plan. "I'll go with you."

We drove to the ferry at Hyannis on March 10 and rode across the gray water to Nantucket, where our closest island friends, Chris and Marybeth, had opened the house for me and were waiting in the living room to greet me.

"I can't believe how happy I am," I told them. "It sounds so strange." Already this magical place was lifting my heart. I had promised the kids a birthday party for Daddy, and we set about planning his perfect celebration.

I woke up to a gray, rainy day on the eleventh. I could smell the sea air, even inside the house. Mark would have been thrilled; the smell of low tide intoxicated him. Audrey was crying that her daddy wouldn't be there to blow out the candles on his birthday cake that evening. But she was easily distracted by the colored paper and stickers I had brought with me so the kids could make birthday cards for Mark, and she set to work with her brother. Rob and I waited all morning for the rain to let up so I could set out with my ashes, but it just kept pouring.

"Let's just go," I finally said.

My first stop was the White Elephant, the beautiful seaside hotel where Mark and I had gotten married. By now, the rain was coming down sideways, freezing cold and relentless. I got out of the car and made my way to the dock where we had posed for our wedding pictures. I climbed down the slippery ladder, crying hysterically, and emptied another packet of Mark's ashes into the water.

"Where to next?" Rob asked back in the car.

"Let's go to New Lane," I answered. That was where we bought our first small place in Nantucket and had enjoyed happy getaways as newlyweds. I assumed the house would be closed for the winter, and Marybeth, who is a realtor, had assured me no one was in residence. I was surprised to see a car in the driveway. "Uh-oh," I muttered. What was the protocol here? Knocking on the door seemed ill-advised. I doubted that even the most hospitable local would exactly welcome a weepy, soaking wet stranger standing on their doorstep off-season to ask for permission to scatter her husband's remains in their backyard. I snuck quietly onto the patio and quickly shook a pinch of Mark's ashes beneath a slender tree under what had been our bedroom window. I didn't want to think about what trespassing statutes I was breaking with that one. I had gone from tragic to ludicrous again.

My next stop was Madaket Marine, where Mark had kept his beloved fishing boat docked. It had been sold the summer before, and his old slip was empty. I watched as more ashes disappeared beneath the water's glassy surface. Finally, I ended up at Dionis Beach, where Mark and I had rented a cottage the summer we were engaged. I walked into the freezing water and let go of him once more.

In town I bought a birthday cake, decorated to look like an ocean, with *Happy Birthday Daddy* written out in blue icing. Carrying the cake to the car, I was struck by the pungent smell in the air. Low tide again. It was odd to catch a whiff of it in town, and odder still that it was lingering so late in the day. Stopping at the wine shop to pick up a bottle of champagne for a bittersweet toast, I could still smell low tide, and I realized it had been there all day, wherever I went. Mark. I knew then that I had found what I had searched for so desperately that first night I returned to Mercer Street. His lost scent.

For his birthday dinner, we ate Mark's favorite lobster bake from Sayle's Seafood—I was relieved to find them open when most of the island was still shuttered for winter. We feasted on lobster, red potatoes, corn, steamed clams, mussels, clam chowder, and the two sides of fried clams that Mark always insisted on ordering. It was stormy all night, but the next morning broke crystal clear, sunny and beautiful, and I woke up with a sense of relief. I had gotten through the birthday. I called for Grouper and got ready to go on my favorite trail run, straight out to the ocean and back through the woods. I made the mistake of turning on my phone first, and saw that my stepfather had forwarded me an e-mail from Andy.

On Mark's birthday, Andy had tried to reach me via e-mail, then reached out to my stepdad to intercede when he got no response. He apparently had been asking Mark's friends where I was, too, and had solved what he perceived to be some sinister mystery.

I've been thinking about you today and what an unbelievable source of strength and comfort you were to Mark, he wrote Marty. *I will always be grateful to you for that and for the support you gave me in our darkest moments. Today has been very difficult for me and I hope you're getting through it without too much sadness . . . It's hard not to think about him all the time.*

I exchanged a few e-mails with Stephanie this week, and it's obvious that she's extremely angry with me. She mentioned that she was going away for the weekend, and when I asked where she was gong [sic] she wouldn't tell me. I found out last night that she was in Nantucket and it dawned on me this morning that perhaps she's up there scattering Mark's ashes. I hope that isn't the case, as I told her that I wanted to be part of that when it happened. I know that Daniel and Kate do too, and they would be devastated i [sic] they missed out on such an important event. Please do what you can to see that she includes us.

I immediately punched in Andy's number, but the call went straight to voice mail. I went for my run. It was windy and cold, but I could sense Mark running alongside me and felt his happiness. I missed him so much. Back at the house, I worried that Kate and Daniel might have been falsely told that I had disposed of their father's remains. There had been no "event." I called their mother to reassure them that this wasn't the case. Susan was guarded but gracious. Yes, Andy had called, she confirmed, but she refused to rush to judgment. "Stephanie, it's your decision," she said kindly. I told her what my intention had been all along: I was dividing the ashes into four equal shares. One for Andy, one each for Kate and Daniel, and the rest for Nick, Audrey, and myself. Susan interrupted before I could go on.

"You're not doing that," she said harshly. "My children won't want that."

Her response surprised me. Surely Ruth would have welcomed the chance to do something with Kate and Daniel to say good-bye and honor Mark's memory in a way that felt right to them. I obviously didn't want to be part of that tableau, but I honestly felt that whatever they chose to do was something that belonged to them. I let Susan say her piece, and silently promised Kate and Daniel that I would safeguard their father's ashes for the day when they were ready to decide for themselves what they wanted to do. Maybe someday Daniel would want to scatter them on a favorite mountainside where his father had taken him snowboarding, or Kate would want to honor him in some private way of her own. My child psychologist had stressed to me how important it was to leave such options open for Nick and Audrey to someday have closure, given how hard that is to find in cases of suicide. If any or all of the children wanted to include me in whatever they chose to do someday, I would be there for them, but just as important, I wanted to respect their privacy.

Later that afternoon, Andy returned my phone message, clearly irate.

"I sent you an e-mail yesterday and you didn't respond," he complained.

"I didn't get one," I said, double-checking. There was a long silence on the other end of the line while Andy scrolled through his e-mails, too.

"I sent it to the wrong address," he said flatly.

"Yes, I'm up in Nantucket," I told him. "You have to respect my privacy. I don't want to have to tell everyone where I am and what I'm doing all the time."

"Like I said at the memorial service, it's up to you to decide what to do with Mark's ashes," Andy reminded me. "I just want to be included."

I explained my decision about dividing the ashes into four equal shares.

"I don't want that," he snapped.

"Well, then fine," I shot back. "But nothing is going to happen for at least ten years, until Audrey and Nick are old enough." If I was going to put together some formal ceremony or another memorial, it was going to be on their terms, to help them heal.

"That's fine." Andy relented. "Even if it's ten years from now, I'm just telling you I want to be included."

I felt exhausted. I couldn't imagine what this tattered family was going to look like in another decade. Would unbearable loss eventually bring us closer, would it be our only bond? Or would we just go our separate ways, rebuild our separate lives, and try to forget how much we had all hurt one another?

When I checked my inbox again, I found another e-mail. This one was from Ruth, dated on her dead son's birthday. The first two sentences acknowledged my pain and said she thought about me constantly. The rest of the brief message was about herself, and how misunderstood she really was.

I don't know really why you are so angry at me, she wrote. *To begin with I need you to know that I knew nothing of what Bernie was doing. When Mark asked me to stop any contact that I had with Bernie I must tell you about what was happening to me. I was totally alone. I was rejected from every apartment. I couldn't go out . . . I was desperately lonely, crying myself to sleep every night and very confused and conflicted. Bernie was the only one I had.*

She recounted her e-mail exchanges with Mark and Andy as the second anniversary of the scandal had approached, and how she was hoping to see them when she visited Kate and Daniel that Christmas. She clearly hadn't accepted Mark's final decision nixing that plan in an e-mail where he told her that he simply wasn't ready to see her again.

I was planning to tell them I needed them too much and that I would stop having anything to do with Bernie, Ruth said. *I truly believe if we had been able to speak to each other, we could have come upon an agreement.*

But so unfortunately, it was too late.

I took a last walk, barefoot on the frozen ground, from our dream house out to the little observation deck where Mark and I used to sit and enjoy the view. It was too foggy to see anything now. Leaving on the noon ferry, we sailed past the White Elephant. Those three days brought back my happiest memories, but the pain of being on the island without him was unbearable. *It will be a very long time before I can come back here,* I told myself as Nantucket disappeared behind the fog.

Back home on Mercer Street, it took two weeks before I could sit down and respond to Ruth's last e-mail. I dissected her single, self-pitying paragraph as if it were a thesis, bitterly tearing apart her arguments point by point.

You could have had me and my children and YOUR children, I reminded her. *You also had Kate and Daniel and Susan. Bernie is all you had? He is in jail. What could Bernie possibly have given you at that point?*

I seized upon a line where she had declared that "my children were the center of my life always and you know that."

Actually, Ruth, no, I don't know that. If they were truly the center of your life, then on the day Bernie confessed his crimes to them you should have left that apartment with them. Again, you chose Bernie.

On and on I railed, filling the screen with my blind rage. Not for one minute did I believe that she had cut off all contact with Bernie, any more than I had bought his similar claim in the letter he had sent from his jail cell a few weeks before. But at this point, I realized, I no longer cared.

I don't have it in me to forgive you for standing by the man who killed my husband, I told her. *Good luck to you Ruth.*

I hit Send and felt the same peacefulness settle over me that I had experienced when I had given up Mark's ashes to the sea.

What needed to be said had been said now, for both of us.

I was done with good-bye.

· *ten* ·

WISH FLOWERS

Nobody knows who I am, but I still hide at first, staking out my favorite bike in the back row. The lights are dim, the music is loud, and our instructor, Laurie, is full of energy and upbeat affirmations. "Get out of your head and into your body!" she urges, and I pedal harder up an invisible hill.

Exercise has always helped me through rough times, but spinning has become more than an endorphin release to me. I go there once, sometimes twice a week. It's forty-five minutes where I don't have to think. Losing weight isn't my goal; I've had no appetite since Mark's death, and the stress has caused me to lose more than twenty pounds already. It's strength I need. Strength and escape.

Sometimes one of the Real Housewives of New York shows up

for a class, too, and we exchange pleasantries. Everything else in my life has become surreal, and it seems oddly fitting that my favorite exercise class is now, too. Even the name is ironic: SoulCycle. I find myself listening eagerly to Laurie's shouts of encouragement. "Let 'em see you sweat! Never let 'em see you struggle!" I seize on her proclamations like the freshest convert at a salvation show. "Leave whatever is not working for you in this room!" Laurie commands as class comes to an end in a final sprint. We climb off our bikes and head back into the blinding sunlight of the real world. I gradually work my way up to a bike in the second row.

Fresh start, new beginning, clean slate: The clichés all make it sound like one big, promising adventure. But building a new life is hard labor. Back in the loft on Mercer Street, Nick and Audrey pick up where they left off, and I envy the innocent way they deal with their loss; they're too young to anticipate pain, or to wallow in it after it broadsides them. People always ask me, brows furrowed in concern, voices dropped to a near whisper, "And how are the kids doing?" The question drives me crazy. "The kids are doing great!" I truthfully reply, thinking to myself, *for now.*

I worry about the years, and questions, yet to come. Audrey doesn't remember her grandfather, and Nick never knew him. I will tell them who he was, what he did to so many innocent people, and how he drove their father to his death when they are mature enough to understand and absorb such horrors. That will mean telling versions of this story over and over to them, filling in the details only as they can handle them. I refuse to let the events of these past two years define them or affect their entire lives.

I'm already sensitive to well-intentioned assumptions. When a caregiver oversympathizes with Nick's separation anxiety, telling me, "Of course, he's had a hard time lately," I bristle. Many of the other two-year-olds in class are clingy, too, and Nick has no idea what happened that morning as he slept in his crib. My children don't know that there's a template for all of this, that there are five stages of loss, academically acclaimed and widely cited. My soul predictably cycles through denial, anger, bargaining, depression, and acceptance and then loops back around again, but children don't follow this route; they don't "process" feelings. They feel them. When sadness hits them, they literally stop in their tracks to react, and then move on.

Audrey goes to the huge windows overlooking Mercer Street and shouts greetings to the sky, confident that her father can hear her. "I love you, I miss you, I kiss you, I squeeze you!" she sings. Nick follows, gleefully mimicking his big sister. "Hi, Daddy! Hi, Daddy!" They happily perform in the window while I cry, not just for Mark anymore, but for what he is missing. They're getting so big now, and so smart, and there are a dozen things that Audrey and Nick say or do every single day that I know Mark would find hilarious, like their Fourth of July underwear march across my parents' front lawn in Montauk.

Montauk was supposed to become our new place together, a replacement for Nantucket. Mark and I had both spent happy summers playing on Montauk beaches when we were growing up, and as long as we avoided Bernie's old haunts later on, Mark seemed to enjoy it. Our last family photo together was taken there on a chilly day just after Thanksgiving. We look like a perfectly normal, happy family.

We had gone to Long Island that weekend to see the holiday lighting of the Montauk Point Lighthouse. As thousands of white lights outlined the lighthouse and keeper's quarters, we listened to a band play Christmas carols and huddled together as the wind bit our faces. I went back six months later with my last little box of ashes. It was Memorial Day weekend, and surfers in their wetsuits were already paddling past the breakers to wait for a perfect wave when I left the house at seven in the morning. I headed for the village, remembering the comic scene the last time Mark and I had driven through. He had been at the wheel when I had suddenly let out a yelp.

"Stop!"

Mark slammed on the brakes and looked at me in alarm. "What?"

I craned my neck around. "It's Alex and Simon and Johan and François!" I cried. My favorite bizarro family from *The Real Housewives of New York*.

Mark rolled his eyes at me. "Oh, God," he said.

I ignored his pointed lack of enthusiasm. "No, no, no! Turn around! I wanna be able to see them!" Mark refused to oblige. He never understood my appetite for the contrived drama. Since becoming part of the all-too-real Madoff drama, I had become hopelessly addicted to the faux hysteria of the Housewives. I tried to rope Mark into it, too, so we could share the sheer comic relief, but he preferred to escape into crime dramas instead. I wanted release; he wanted resolution.

I went to the Montauk Bake Shoppe, a favorite ritual of ours that always drove Ruth crazy when Mark and I were staying at the Madoffs' beach house. "Don't you dare bring those back here!" she would scold us as we made our daily coffee run, knowing we'd come back loaded with pastries. Smiling at the memory, I went up to the counter and placed our usual order.

"Four fried jelly croissants, three blueberry muffins, one raspberry scone, one blueberry scone, and two cookies, please." Nick and Audrey loved the M&M eyes on the fish-shaped cookies. I took a large cup of coffee to go and made my way to the lighthouse. The point where the lighthouse sits is known as The End by locals, and as a kid, I always thought the Montauk lighthouse marked where the world ended. The magnetic moon was always trying to pull the earth away, I had learned in science classes, but we held fast. Water, however, couldn't resist the tug, and the romance between moon and sea played out in the rise and fall of the tide. The End, I reasoned, must be the very spot where we clung to the world.

I hiked down the steep path to the rocky shore beneath the lighthouse and sat on a large boulder, balancing my cup of coffee between the wet stones. The lighthouse horn bleated and I watched the sun glint off the fishing boats leaving Block Island Sound for the Atlantic. The morning felt fresh and rinsed clean, like sheets drying on a clothesline, and I wondered how Mark could willingly leave this world when there was so much beauty to take in. Did he really think he could not find happiness in anything again? I peered down at the crystal shallows and saw a tiny heart-shaped rock, like the ones Nick and Audrey had been hunting for in vain all weekend. I picked it up and put it in my pocket. I took out the last plastic packet of ashes and kissed it, then emptied it into the glittering sea.

"Hope you have fun fishing," I said. The bluefish, flounder, and striped bass were known to be bountiful in the rip where the bay meets the ocean. I climbed back up the cliff and hurried home with the box of treats, willing myself to be happy and present. Audrey and Nick deserved that much, I knew. I was just beginning to realize that I did, too.

EPILOGUE

Getting us out of the apartment where Mark killed himself was my biggest priority and my greatest frustration. I had gone back to my wistful online searches of real-estate listings, taking virtual tours of homes where I could imagine a swing set in the backyard and squirrels for Grouper to chase and barbecues with neighbors who had no clue that I was once a Madoff.

I fell in love with a small slice of lakefront property in Armonk, one of the little towns in Westchester County that I had begged Mark to consider for our new beginning. I drove up to look at the lot. The street was leafy and quiet, just a short drive from the elementary school. My graduate school would be a shorter commute than I had now from SoHo, and there were a few hospitals in the area where I could apply for jobs once I finished my degree in the spring of 2013. We would enjoy a simple, normal life. The lot had only a foundation so far, but I liked the idea of building something from the ground up. Greenwich was just minutes away, which would make it easier for

Kate and Daniel to remain in our lives. Maybe Charlie the crane could find us, too, if he had survived the cruel winter as we did.

I discreetly listed the loft for rent, and was encouraged when one of the first couples to see it instantly wanted to sign a lease. They just as quickly opted out once they discovered whose apartment it was and what had happened here. The Madoff name alone had chased off potential renters the summer before, when we had tried to lease out the Nantucket house for the season. Knowing how unjustly damned Mark felt, I am left to wonder what it will take, beyond his very life, to convince the lynch mob that we shared Bernie's name, not his morality.

My ties to the shattered Madoff family are thin and fragile, like a thread pulled taut. Andy popped in and out of our lives like a cameo player who had been handed the wrong script. He would ask on short notice to see the kids, then come up to the apartment and sit at the dining room table or on the fireplace ledge just watching us, saying little or, sometimes, nothing. I felt as if we were under observation. He never brought his own two girls to see their young cousins, nor did he offer to take his niece and nephew out to play in a park, or maybe to see the dinosaurs at the museum. Nick's second birthday went unmentioned by his uncle, but I received an e-mail from Andy the following day informing me that he was canceling our health insurance through the alternative-energy company he and Mark had cofounded. At the same time, I had to temper my own anger, because he was the trustee of Mark's estate and I had to depend on him continuing to act in good faith. I felt bad that he had to deal with such a mess.

Andy and I never knew quite what to make of each other; rage and sorrow were the only things we had in common anymore. I don't know what he wants of me, but I do know that I am done trying to please any Madoffs. And so Mark's brother and I dance around each other like two wary, wounded old boxers. When he leaves my apartment, he often contacts my stepfather or brother to criticize me and to express his supposed concern for me: I've lost too much weight, he will report, or I seem mentally unstable. The latter diagnosis at least gave Marty a good chuckle when he heard how it came about. I had threatened aloud to call Irving Picard's office and leave a prank message claiming to be Lindsay Lohan or Britney Spears. Marty, unlike Andy, immediately got the joke, and knew it was just a funny fantasy about how to goad the trustees into returning my lawyer's calls.

Andy was also obsessing over my plans to go public with my story. "You'll hurt yourself, you'll hurt your children, and you'll hurt me," he warned.

"I'm doing this *for* my children," I reiterated. "And for Mark. Stop harassing me."

He turned his campaign to my stepfather and my friends.

"This will bankrupt her," he told a friend of mine. "We have a PR agency that is trying to keep our name out of the press because people hate us." Publicity, he argued, would only hurt the attempts to reach a settlement in the lawsuits.

Andy's logic didn't seem to apply to himself. Catherine had appointed herself "family spokesman" as soon as Bernie was arrested, even though she had been introduced to all of us only several months before. In the aftermath of Bernie's downfall, Catherine used the Madoff name as often as possible in promoting her disaster-preparedness business. Andy was often seen at her side, on TV and in magazines and newspapers.

He tried a different strategy with my stepfather, asking Marty to meet him for a drink one afternoon. Andy told Marty he was worried that I was losing it. Marty thanked him for his concern and told him my grief was overwhelming, but I was learning to deal with it: I had a support system of family, friends, and a trusted therapist, and he didn't need to worry about me or the kids. Andy then brought up my publishing plans and his fear of any publicity. Marty asked why he didn't object to Catherine's eagerness to be interviewed or quoted, or to use the Madoff name to get attention for her business.

"Yeah," he replied lamely, "we are cutting back on publicity that mentions me. Phasing me out PR-wise."

Throughout it all, I still took him at his word that he wanted to forge some kind of relationship with Nick and Audrey, and I let the odd visits continue. During one of them, as I was getting ready to leave for school, he badgered me about a specific watch of Mark's that Daniel had asked me for shortly after his father's death. "I feel so bad," I had told Daniel, "but your dad had it engraved for Nicholas when he was born. But I'm happy to give you another one." I hadn't had the heart yet to sort through Mark's belongings. When I recounted our conversation for Andy, he wanted proof that the watch was engraved with Nick's name.

"Can I see it?" he asked.

Near tears, I brought it out and showed him my son's name and birth date etched on the back.

"I have every intention of giving Kate and Daniel some of their father's belongings," I said. I pulled another watch from Mark's cherished collection and put it on the dining room table, then looked for something to send to Kate, settling on a wedding band Mark had bought from a silversmith at her summer camp.

"I'm not ready to part with these yet, but here, you go ahead and take them," I said. I grabbed my bag and rushed for the door before I broke down.

"Susan, wait!" Andy called after me.

I whipped around. "It's *Stephanie*," I said, and left.

Several weeks afterward, Andy was halfway out the door at the end of one of his visits when he casually announced that Kate and Daniel wanted to see Nick and Audrey, but had insisted he be present because they felt uncomfortable around me, "because of the book." I was stung. I had taken Kate out to lunch and shopping in the city for her sixteenth birthday just a month earlier, and we had had a great time. Troubled by Andy's assertion, I sat down the next morning to write both kids an e-mail, asking if I had done something to upset them, and assuring them that they were loved and always welcome to visit. Daniel immediately sent back a warm reply, and the three of us made arrangements to get together in Greenwich on an upcoming weekend.

When the day arrived, the kids showed up around lunchtime, texting me beforehand to ask if I wanted anything from their favorite chicken joint. Kate immediately plopped down to play with Nick and Audrey, who basked in her attention, and I was surprised when Daniel settled in to talk with me. Kate and I had always been close in a girly way, while Daniel, who is three years older, had regarded both Mark and me with typical teenaged disdain. The two of them stayed at the house for a few hours, and we chatted about their friends and their plans for the summer, never daring to plunge into the deeper waters of what we had all been through these past two and a half years. Daniel politely asked if he could have some of his father's old fishing gear.

"Of course," I told him, biting my tongue when he came back downstairs later with the entire lot. I longed to reclaim at least one reel for Nicholas to have as a keepsake someday, but I didn't know how to ask. And if Daniel found some measure of comfort in the collection of lovingly used rods and reels, I would never take even a fraction of that away from him.

Kate wanted a few family photos and laid claim to some autographed baseball bats. Daniel then launched into a story about a luxurious yacht he had once been aboard, which had belonged to a friend of Papa Bernie. It was jarring to hear the old term of endearment for his felon grandfather. I was surprised, but shouldn't have been. Ruth and Bernie had never been cut off from Kate and Daniel as decisively as our children now were. I half wondered if they would be going to North Carolina to visit Papa Bernie someday; Daniel was already old enough to make the choice for himself, and Kate wasn't far behind. I never heard either of them express any hurt, anger, or shame about what their grandfather had done; in Greenwich, they were seen, rightfully, as innocent victims, and the attention appeared to be purely positive and supportive. Kate had no problem competing in national swim meets with the name Madoff up on the scoreboards for all to see; I admired her stoicism.

The dynamic has shifted for the adults, as well. Ruth was the subject of a sympathetic profile in *People* magazine, which took note of the incognito life she was living down in Florida, driving a used car and volunteering to help the homeless. Even Andy had migrated back to his mother's side. "I've seen my mom, and it's actually been really nice," he had told me one afternoon.

"That's nice," I replied vaguely. Maybe that was what was behind the awkward visits; using Andy as a conduit to try to work her way back into my children's lives would be a classic Ruth maneuver. I have to admire her tenacity even as I resent her for failing to instill that same scrappy determination in her oldest son.

I do still think of Ruth often. I don't regret my decision at all to honor Mark's wishes, but I wonder if I will ever face her again. My heart softens and hardens.

I learned through a newspaper story that Catherine and a friend of hers are publishing a book, apparently about "one of the most controversial figures of our time," and I can only assume that Andy Madoff is attached to it somehow. Andy's scurrying about to ensure my silence makes sense. His sudden new devotion to his brother's younger children and his odd visits also make sense: We *were* being observed. I had been played by a Madoff again.

Every Friday, I trek uptown with Audrey to see a child life specialist who's been helping me navigate these new waters. We stop for a black-and-white cookie at the deli on the corner before going to see Sallie. "Keep Mark present," was her first advice to me about helping Nick and Audrey. What breaks my heart heals theirs. Their nightstands each hold two or three photographs of their father, and I sometimes find them clutching one in a small hand as they sleep.

I lost my own biological father suddenly, when he died of an aneurysm on the night of my high school graduation. I was eighteen. I started my summer job the next day. I had loved him, but my parents were divorced and my father and I had never forged a close bond. Still, I knew what it felt like to lose a parent unexpectedly, and I wanted to preserve Mark's memory for our children in a healthy way.

On Audrey's first visit, Sallie had shown her how to trace her hand, then color each finger a different color and write a message for her father on each one. "I went to ballet class with Scarlett today," she wants him to know. "Ella came over to play." She is pleased that she can still tell her daddy whatever she wants, and she relays her news to him with drawings and Post-it notes stuck to our windows, so Mark can read them from the sky.

Sallie also suggested we start a memory book to keep the pictures Nick and Audrey draw for their father, the things they say, and my own notes about what he was like. I bought a huge black leather album and had it embossed with the words DADDY'S MEMORY BOOK, and stockpile little notepads in bright, cheery colors for me to write down all of Mark's favorite things: Daddy's favorite candies were Chuckles, orange slices, Milk Duds, and orange circus peanuts. Daddy's favorite restaurant was Blue Ribbon, because he loved their paella. Daddy's favorite foods for Mommy to cook were lasagna, roast chicken, and fried breaded flounder. Daddy's favorite movie was *The Hangover*. I pull up every detail I can remember and create list after list.

I also include two letters on Snoopy stationery that Mark wrote from sleepaway camp in Pennsylvania when he was eleven years old. *Dear Mom,* he wrote in the first, *Each Friday we have a social. I don't know what to do. I don't like camp because everybody talks about girls . . .* And then a second, briefer missive: *Dear Mom, I'm coming home with you on visiting day so bring the big car. Love, Mark.* They crack me up, and I recognize in Nick already the same budding athleticism his father had. How Mark would have loved seeing himself in his own little boy. Whenever the kids say something cute or funny or tender about Mark, I run for a notepad and write it down to put in the black album. It feels like I'm keeping a baby book.

"My daddy taught me how to play the yo-yo."

"You know, my daddy used to let me pee in the beach water."

"My dad is a really good driver."

"I miss the Towel Monster."

I try to become the Towel Monster, putting a towel on my own head at bath time, but I stop because it feels too sacred. The Towel Monster belonged to him; it should be just theirs. Trying to fill the void, I learn, only underscores its presence.

Sallie recommended a suicide survivors' support group for me, but I demurred. I still have scary flashbacks from a new-mother group I joined after Audrey was born. I thought I was going to make new friends and discuss sleep-training, but the half-dozen other mommies in the group had all known one another socially already, and their chumminess was hard to penetrate. I felt intimidated. They spent the hour bitching about their husbands and their renovations. I never opened my mouth. My husband was my best friend, and I liked my kitchen appliances and master-bath fixtures just fine, too. "I'm good," I tell Sallie.

And I am, more and more often. When an old friend from high school runs into me on the street and suggests we get together for drinks, I happily agree, then change my mind by the time I get home. Does he know what happened to me? And if not, do I want to tell him? I text him asking for a rain check. We reschedule, and I make another excuse, but by the third time I feel guilty and just go. I end up having a great time laughing and reminiscing, and Stephanie Madoff and her tragedy never come up. Friends from grad school invite me out, too, and I go through the same routine.

Weekends are always the toughest for me, when I am the loneliest. Mark and I spent all our free time together; Saturday and Sunday were the highlights of my week. Now I dread them. But looking back doesn't make me feel any better. Having fun is still an effort, but I'm more willing to make it than I was just a few months ago. I even go to a restaurant I love but have been avoiding because it brings back memories of a romantic date Mark and I had during a Saturday-night blizzard.

The restaurant was a popular one, and getting a table was impossible. But as snow blanketed the city that night, Mark and I had the sudden inspiration to make our way from 72nd Street clear downtown to Il Buco, reasoning that no one else would venture out in this weather and we could finally score a table. Mark, ever the sensible one, called first to make sure they were open. We arrived shivering and shaking snow from our boots, but triumphant. The restaurant was cozy and warm, and we ate the most delicious pork chops in the known universe, and topped our meal off with a dessert wine and a panna cotta drizzled with balsamic vinegar.

Returning nervously with friends on a rainy summer evening seven months after Mark's suicide, I ordered the exact same meal, laughed with my friends, and savored every morsel.

I started to miss volunteering at the hospital and look forward to the internship I had to postpone for a year. There must be new families on the pediatric floor now. I wonder how they're coping.

One day, Audrey balled up her small fist and started hitting herself in the head.

"Audrey, stop doing that! You're going to hurt yourself, silly," I chided her. "I don't like to see that."

"Okay," she promised agreeably.

I caught her doing it again.

"Aw, I forgot," she apologized brightly. "You don't want me to do it!"

The third time, I finally got it.

"Are you trying to give your brain a boo-boo so you can see your daddy again?" I asked. This is all she knows about Mark's death: Sometimes people get a boo-boo on the brain and it makes their brain stop working, which makes their heart stop working, and when your heart stops working, your body dies.

"Yes," she answered.

"No," I told her. "That's not going to happen. I know this is very hard and sad. But you are never going to be able to see Daddy again. But you will always be able to feel him with your heart."

And she does understand, I know. When she started to learn how to write, she printed her name neatly on scraps of paper and the pictures of flowers she likes to draw. She asked how to spell *Daddy* and practiced until she could do it perfectly, except for a stubbornly backward *y*. She asked how to spell *die*. It was the first verb she learned to write. *Daddy Die* she labels everything.

The flowers she draws are surprisingly precise for a four-year-old, and I compliment her on the lovely petals and perfectly proportioned stems. She colors most of them pink, her favorite color.

"It's a wish flower," she tells me. She got the idea from a cartoon show where characters were blowing on dandelions and making wishes.

"What are you wishing for?" I ask her.

"Daddy to come back," she replies.

It's been six months and a thousand times that I've had to disappoint her, but the psychologists all agree it's important to be consistent and clear, so I draw a deep breath and tell her again that her daddy is never coming back.

"I know," she says too wisely. "It's just pretend."

No, I say to myself. *It's not.*

I found an apartment to rent in another downtown neighborhood, close to the kids' school. Miraculously, I was able to lease out the Mercer Street loft, and prepared to move out and move on.

From the master closet, I gathered up Mark's clothes and packed separate boxes for Kate, Daniel, and myself. I selected shirts, hats, and ties that are meaningful to each of us—the button-down shirt he wore to Daniel's high school graduation, the tie he wore to Kate's bat mitzvah. Just when I thought I'd finished, feeling drained, I remembered the hall closet full of Mark's coats and steeled myself for another round. I laughed when I found a neatly folded plastic dog-poop bag in every single coat pocket.

I kept sorting and packing. I put some of my own things into a box I labeled MEMORY CLOTHES. There's the white sweater with crystals that I wore to our rehearsal dinner, and the fancy evening sandals I bought for our big date to the long-ago STANY dinner. I preserved a little bottle of coconut-mango shampoo from our romantic vacation on Little Palm Island, but then I unpacked it again and threw it away.

The new tenants are insisting I remove the big wooden fish bolted to the study wall, and I'm assuming they'll want to banish the shellacked dusky shark whose fin is forever threatening to poke out an unsuspecting visitor's eye in the front hallway, too. I don't want these things now, either. Most everything from this place, this life, will go into storage. I'm only taking our beds, our clothes, the kids' toys, some dishes, our pictures, the memory book, and the matte black metal box. What I truly need, and what I truly cherish.

All the rest, I'm leaving behind.

ACKNOWLEDGMENTS

When I decided to write this book, I had no idea how I would feel in the weeks, months, even years after making my choice. It was far harder to do than I could ever have anticipated, and it was a horrendously painful process at times. And, at times, it was the best therapy I could ask for. I'm very grateful to the people who worked with me to tell this story: Tammy Jones, a truly gifted writer and interviewer, who spent many, many patient hours with me on the manuscript, and who will forever be a friend; my editor, Sarah Hochman, who guided us both and who has been my rock every step of the way; my publisher, David Rosenthal, who embraced this book in its initial stages and gave it all of his support; associate publisher Aileen Boyle, who navigated publicity and marketing so deftly; and the team at Blue Rider Press and Penguin USA, whose belief in my book was encouraging in even the darkest hours.

Tremendous thanks are also due to my agent, Steve Troha, and to my publicist, RoseMarie Terenzio, who both worked tirelessly on my behalf.

My stepdad, Martin London, made invaluable contributions along the way, and I am eternally grateful for his love, devotion, and guidance. He loved Mark as a son, and in the midst of his own heartbreak has helped and advised me in the face of continuing challenges and conflict every day.

Thank you to my wonderful and loving family: Mom, Rob, Sloane, Wilke, Jesse, Liz, Aunt Karen, and my cousins Beth, Meg, Amy, and Jo (Yes, they are named after *Little Women*!). And thank you to Daniel and Kate Madoff for being such a great older brother and sister to Audrey and Nicholas.

Thank you to my dear friends Christi Friedman, RoseMarie Terenzio, Ronit Berkman, Joe and Courtney Goldsmith, and Jennifer Nilles, whom I needed most when Mark died and who spent countless hours and days at my side.

Many thanks are also due to so many friends who have supported my family and me wonderfully through these past few years: the staff at 158 Mercer Street (John, Miguel, Floyd, Igor, Steve, and Julio), Penny and Chris Armstrong, Bill Berkman, Matt Berman, Gabi Brand, Toni Calamari, Josie Carvajal, Nancy Chemtob, the Child Life crew at Bank Street College of Education (Beth Braddy, Lesley Frankel, Sharon Granville, Emily Johnson, Caitlin Koch, Marissa Madigan-Keane, Mariel Maffetone, Leslie Marnett, Elena Michaelcheck, Oana Orodelo, Troy Pinkney-Ragsdale, Diane Rode, Lee Russeth, Camille Soto, Stefani Tower, Deb Vilas, Alix Watson, and Hillary Woodward), CLS Team at MSKCC (Therese Weisbrot, Jessica Annenberg, Alyson Silver, and Evan Clarke), Nei Cruz, J.T. Danielson, Samantha Diedrick, Andrew Ehrlich, Dr. Marc Engelbert (as well as Karen and Diana), Leila

ACKNOWLEDGMENTS

Fazel, Martin Flumenbaum, Josh Forman, Christina Franzese, Tracy Frost, Liz Georgantas, Emily Gershon, Marybeth and Chris Gibson, Debbie Perelman-Gil and Gideon Gil, Aaron Goldschmidt, Bob and Sandie Greene, Haven Spa (Marta, Yasmine, Rebecca, Fahmida, Ira, Emma, and Gabi), Justin and Merrilou Hillenbrand, Dorothy Hutcheson, Jennifer James, Kathy Kalesti, Rachel Karliner, Ph.D., Laura Kosin, Keith Lascalea, Daniel and Michelle Lehmann, Lure Fishbar (Josh, Robert, Albert, Lisa, Roz, and John), Petal McDonald, Mariana Meja (and Karen), Mark Merriman, Brenda Mikel, Sandy Miller, Brian Milton, Michael Olajide, Jack O'Neil, Lilia Parkes, Danny Pfeffer, Katia Pryce, Mary Risi, Narciso Rodriguez, Francesca Santorelli-Breheney, Sallie Sandborn, Maria Seremetis, Hannah Sholl, Errol Sibley, Adam Stracher, Tom Tolan, Agata Wachulska, Washington Market School (Ronnie, Joan, Chelsea, Kim, and Maria), Susan Wilen, and Jen and Josh Wilkes.

My heartfelt thanks to Jacky Marshall for her generous permission to include several of her beautiful photographs inside the book and on the front jacket.

Photo insert: pages 2 (bottom left and right), 3, 4, and 5 (top) courtesy Jacky Marshall